A Guide to Research in American Library History

by

Michael H. Harris

The Scarecrow Press, Inc.

Metuchen, N.J.   1968

For Linda

Preface

This book is intended to serve four purposes: (1) to indicate areas of darkness and light in the broad spectrum of research in American library history; (2) to discuss the philosophy and methodology used by American library historians; (3) to provide a descriptive list of the guides to primary and secondary source materials that are of use to the library historian; and (4) to present a descriptive bibliography of the nearly five hundred masters theses and doctoral dissertations on American library history completed through 1965.

Anyone who has studied American library history is aware of the contribution of graduate research to our understanding of the development of libraries in this country. This book is intended to encourage and facilitate further studies of this type, not only by graduate library school students but also by graduate students working towards degrees in American history, literature, and education.

This book will also serve the professional historian, who has neglected this significant area of American intellectual history, and the practicing librarian, who has failed to take much interest in his own history. Hopefully this volume will remove some of the roadblocks the librarian and historian encounter in undertaking research in American library history.

The author of a book of this type, which is based primarily on the research of others, owes many debts. I wish to acknowledge my debt to Dr. Ralph Shaw, who encouraged the germ of an idea that grew into a book and gave prompt and intelligent advice as it progressed; to Dr. Gladys Spargo of Northern Illinois University, who patiently listened to my impromptu lectures on American library history; to Dr. Jesse Shera, Western Reserve University, who has contributed so much to the writing of American library history, and who gave freely of his time to discuss the subject with this writer; to Dr. Louis Shores, Florida State University, who has shown a continuing interest in this project; to Dr. Haynes McMullen and Dr. Peter Hiatt of Indiana University, who read the first part of the book in a characteristically painstaking manner and offered many helpful suggestions as to its improvement; and to many more who know their important contributions to the completion of this book. Of course, any errors or misinterpretations remaining are only my own.

I gratefully acknowledge my debt to the staff of the libraries at the University of Chicago, University of Illinois, and Western Reserve University. Their prompt and courteous service to a visiting scholar on a tight timetable was greatly appreciated. A great debt is owed Mrs. Mathews, interlibrary loan librarian at Indiana University Library. My excessive demands were always met with kind and efficient service. My thanks to Mrs. Jeremy Jones, who typed a meticulous copy of the manuscript and corrected a number of grammatical errors.

No list of acknowledgments would be complete without special reference to my wife, Linda Jo Harris, who has given up several vacations in support of her husband's determination to study library history, and has contributed much to whatever merits this book may claim.

Contents

Part One

Part Two

I
American Library History: The State of the Art

The American librarian has shown little interest in the history of libraries and librarianship in this country. Felix Reichmann wondered about this lack of historical interest and concluded, in a recent paper on historical research in library science:

> On the one hand, we (librarians) have a dark suspicion that historical studies are a waste of time, mere 'dates.'   We do like the word pioneer; we share the love of this phrase with American educators, and we are all continuously pioneering in reading services, in technical services, in the application of machines, and so forth.   The pioneer, of course, does not have the time nor the interest to look backwards; for him the past is dead and of no consequence, and his main attention is focused on the future.[1]

It would seem that the attitude of librarians is still limited by what Butler termed "the simplicity of their pragmatism," since they have shown little appreciation for the research and writing of library history.[2]

Unfortunately most writers in the area of intellectual history, men who should be concerned with the library as a social and cultural agency, have neglected library history. However some of America's best historians have been among the small minority that has recognized the significance of the library.   Louis B. Wright contributed much to our understanding of Colonial library history,[3] and Daniel Boorstein gave considerable coverage to library development and reading tastes in his book The Americans: The Colonial Experience, which won the Bancroft Prize in 1959.[4]   Merle Curti treated the development of libraries in his Pulitzer Prize book The Growth of American Thought, and wrote, the library is "one of the most distinctive and influential agencies of our cultural life."[5]

9

One reason for the historians' lack of interest is that
cultural and intellectual history, of which library history is
a part, is relatively new on the American history scene.[6]
Another reason put forth by one historian is that the historical profession has left the field to those who could most
logically be expected to write library history--the professional librarian.[7]

An often implied, but seldom stated, reason for the
neglect of library history is the difficulty involved in this
type of research. The problem was nicely put by Mary
Reed in the preface to her thesis, History of the Lakewood
Public Library, when she wrote:

> This record contributes to the understanding
> of the events described, it seems to me,
> little more than an ornithologist's anatomi-
> cal sketch contributes, say, to fathoming the
> flight of a swallow. The essential questions
> remain. Where is the measure of the tang-
> ible and intangible (effect) of one sentence
> out of the nine million or so books borrowed
> by the people of Lakewood from their li-
> brary during these twenty-five years?[8]

Historians have always found it difficult if not impossible to
assess the influence of books and libraries in terms of directly traceable evidence.

> Whatever the reason for neglect it is obvious that
> library history has been for the most part for-
> gotten by historians of American thought and
> culture, and librarians have in general failed
> to fill in the void left by the followers of Clio.
> The field of library history is wide open; it
> is in every way a legitimate field for scholar-
> ly research and writing. . .and yet barely a
> handful of really competent enterprising souls
> are working in the field.[9]

This recent assessment of the numbers of active library historians in this country is accurate, yet there has been a
large body of historical research done in this field. If it is
not being produced by the professional historian or librarian,
who is doing it?

One need only look at the best monographic studies

on American library history to see that most of them were
originally written as theses or dissertations in library schools
or history departments.

A few examples will illustrate this point. Two of
the best studies of public library development in this country, Jesse Shera's Foundations of the Public Library[10] and
Sidney Ditzion's Arsenals of a Democratic Culture,[11] were
originally dissertations written at Chicago and Columbia re-
spectively. The most useful surveys of academic library
history, Louis Shores' The Origins of the College Library[12]
and Kenneth Brough's Scholar's Workshop,[13] were first written as dissertations at George Peabody and Stanford. Most
of the quality biographies of American librarians, such as
James Holley's Charles Evans[14] and William Frederick
Poole[15] by William Williams, were originally prepared to
meet the requirements for the doctorate in library science.

A list of excellent studies of American library history emanating from graduate library schools and history departments could continue for pages. Of course, all graduate research has not been of this high quality. However,
even the less superior research is better than most of the
studies produced outside the graduate schools. Graduate
students at least receive some basic training in the historical method, work under the guidance of a major advisor,
and are required to meet more or less exacting standards.[16]

Unfortunately many graduate library schools have
chosen to drop the master's thesis as a requirement for the
degree. The lack of qualified faculty to guide such research
and the ever-growing enrollments are reasons often cited.
The loss of this experience is serious to a profession long
characterized by its lack of research ability.

There are, however, a number of library schools
still producing good masters research and American library
history continues to be a popular topic. In 1966, library
school students wrote more than 20 master's theses on
American library history; several are written each year in
departments of education, literature, and history.[17]

American library history has always been a popular
topic for doctoral dissertations. Of the 224 dissertations
abstracted in Library Science Dissertations,[18] 38 were on
American library history, and this list omitted several
titles. Of the eleven doctoral dissertations written in library

11

schools in 1965-66, four were on American library history.

Despite this activity, the landscape of American library history offers large areas of virgin soil to be plowed. Few areas have been exhausted, and many important areas have been totally neglected. A few specific comments on needs and strengths might be of use.

With the large number of topics available, few attempts at re-examination and revision of earlier research are made. However with every passing year it becomes easier to test earlier conclusions. For instance, twenty years ago it would have been impossible to question the validity of the arguments regarding the causal factors responsible for the development of the public library in the East. Today, with the ever-increasing number of histories covering local library development in New England and the Middle Atlantic states, such a test might well be possible.[19] There are dozens of old anniversary histories, frequently showing more sentiment than scholarship, that are badly in need of revision.[20]

General studies, which synthesize earlier, more specific studies, have been rare in American library history. Some historians argue that there are too many gaps in the coverage offered by the local studies, that there just are not enough blocks available to use in the construction of good general histories. However, a number of historically sound (if not well written) local studies are appearing each year, and if the time for the writing of broader histories has not arrived, it will be here soon.

Jesse Shera recently issued a call for a shift in emphasis to the history of librarianship, and away from the history of individual libraries.[21]

> The history of librarianship...treats of the
> changes within the library and the impact of
> those changes upon the services of the library
> as one agency in the communication process...
> The kind of historical writing for which we
> are here arguing would throw a strong light
> on librarianship today, and provide us with
> insight at a time when insight is sorely need-
> ed...Not until such studies have been made
> can the profession speak with authority of
> the meaning of librarianship within its coeval
> culture.[22]

12

Shera stresses the need for studies of librarianship in general, also of particular phases of librarianship such as the development of reference services, cataloging and classification, or special librarianship. [23]

The reading tastes and the private libraries of early Americans have received little attention from library historians. Over the years private library development in New England, [24] the Middle Atlantic States, [25] and the South [26] has been covered relatively well by historians, but the history of private libraries in the rest of the country has yet to be written. [27]

The development of the predecessors of the public library--especially social and commercial circulating libraries--needs extensive further coverage. Good studies of social library development are available for New England, [28] Pennsylvania, [29] California, [30] and Kentucky, [31] but their development elsewhere remains largely untouched.

Public library history has been the most popular topic for research, but considering the thousands of public libraries in this country, the percentage covered is small indeed. Some historians argue that since public library development in all parts of this country paralleled public library development in New England, which has been carefully covered, there is no need for further studies in other parts of the country. Others maintain that we do not know all that is necessary about American public library history--especially in the Middle West, West, and South--and that the question must remain open until much more evidence is in.

Many of the studies were completed as thesis research in graduate library schools, and the subjects tend to be clustered around the library schools involved. More than 35 public libraries in Ohio and 15 in Pennsylvania have been covered by students at Western Reserve and Drexel. Large gaps still remain in the historical coverage of public library development in this country, especially in the West, and this area deserves the attention of library historians.

Next to public libraries, the most popular topic for research has been the college and university library. Nevertheless the number of academic libraries still not covered is legion and far too few regional or national studies have been attempted. Studies that consider the developing significance of the academic library to higher education in this country are badly needed, but are far more difficult to prepare than the usual chronological sketches so prevalent today.

The history of school and special library development has also been neglected by historians. A few scattered studies of local school libraries are available, and several useful state and regional studies have been completed, but much remains to be done. Our knowledge of special library development in this country is just as incomplete. Recently a study of business and industrial library history was completed at the University of Michigan, [32] but it covers only one phase of the subject.

The development of special government libraries also needs study, as Robert Williams indicated in a recent article on federal government libraries:

> The history of government libraries is an important part of the history of American special libraries, and therefore deserves special consideration by library historians...No comprehensive history of federal government libraries has been written, and in most cases even the history of important individual libraries has been ignored. [33]

Writing in 1963, James Holley argued that there were only four biographies of American librarians that could be classed as "scholarly monographs that really interpret the lives of American library pioneers."[34] Since that time only one study has appeared that is worthy of addition to his list. [35] All five studies were completed as doctoral research, and three of them have since been published. A number of shorter studies are available, but most of them are sentimental chronicales lacking a critical approach. The need is great for in-depth scholarly studies of the many important American librarians.[36]

Finally, the history of library associations in this country is still far from complete. In 1963 R. B. Downs indicated the significance of this area when he wrote; "Unquestionably, the work of library associations has been and continues to be a major factor in the development of librarianship."[37] A few histories of state and regional associations are now available, but no one has yet tried to assess the development and influence of the powerful national associations such as the American Library Association and the Special Libraries Association. [37]

In this brief essay it has been impossible to do more

14

than mention the areas in American library history that need
further research, and only a few of the more significant studies could be cited in the footnotes. The reader should take
note of Chapter III of this work, which includes a list of
bibliographical essays and selective bibliographies that evaluate much of the published literature of American library history.

Notes

1. Felix Reichmann, "Historical Research and Library Science," Library Trends, 13:37, 1964.
2. Pierce Butler, Introduction to Library Science. Chicago,
   University of Chicago Press, 1964. p. vii.
3. Wright's books in this area include The First Gentlemen
   of Virginia. Charlottesville, University Press of Virginia,
   1964, first published in 1940. Culture on the Moving Frontier.
   Bloomington, Indiana University Press, 1955 and The Cultural
   Life of the American Colonies, 1607-1763. New York, Harper, 1957.
4. New York, Vintage Books, 1958.
5. Merle Curti, Foreword to Sidney Ditzion's Arsenals of a
   Democratic Culture. Chicago, American Library Association, 1947. p. viii.
6. Richard A. Bartlett, "The State of the Library History
   Art," John David Marshall (ed.) Approaches to Library
   History. Tallahassee, Florida, Journal of Library History.
   1966. p. 20.
   Bartlett makes some interesting comments on the state of
   the art in his criticism of the published histories of American library history but overlooks many of the most significant studies.
7. Ibid.
8. Mary Martha Reed, History of the Lakewood Public Library
   (Unpublished master's thesis). Western Reserve University,
   1958.
9. Bartlett, op. cit., p. 13-14.
10. Chicago, University of Chicago Press, 1949.
11. Chicago, American Library Association, 1947.
12. New York, Barnes and Noble, 1935.
13. Urbana, University of Illinois Press, 1953.
14. Urbana, University of Illinois Press, 1963.
15. New York, Columbia University Press, 1963.
16. Frank Sessa, "Public Library History," in John David
    Marshall (ed.) In Pursuit of Library History. Tallahasee,
    Florida State University Library School, 1961. p. 19.
17. Janet P. Jaffe, "Theses and Reports Accepted by Graduate
    Library Schools, 1965-66," Library Quarterly. 36:325-332,
    1966.

18. Nathan M. Cohen, Barbara Denison, and Jessie C. Boehlert, Library Science Dissertations; 1925-60: An Annotated Bibliography of Doctoral Studies. Washington, Government Printing Office, 1963.
19. An example of such an approach is Ruth L. Giddings The West Hartford Public Library (Unpublished master's thesis, Southern Connecticut State College, 1965) in which the author attempts to analyze the development of the West Hartford Public Library to see if the influences there correspond with general trends as evidenced in published histories of other public libraries.
20. David Mead, "Popular Education and Cultural Agencies," in John Francis McDermott (ed.) Research Opportunities in American Cultural History. Lexington, University of Kentucky Press, 1961. p. 155-167. This essay offers many ideas on research needs in American library history.
21. Jesse Shera, "What the Historian Has Been Missing," Wilson Library Bulletin 40:639, 1966.
22. Ibid.
23. Shera cites Samuel Rothstein The Development of Reference Services Through Academic Traditions, Public Library Practice and Special Librarianship. Chicago, Association of College and Reference Libraries, 1955, as an excellent study of this type.
24. A well done study of the reading interests and private libraries in New England is Thomas Goddard Wright Literary Culture in Early New England, 1620-1730. New Haven, Yale University Press, 1920.
25. Much of the research has been centered on Pennsylvania, the excellent papers and books by Frederick B. Tolles and by Edwin Wolf, 2nd being the most useful.
26. Virginia is by far the best covered of the Southern states for this period.
27. One exception is John Francis McDermott's study of reading and private libraries in St. Louis, Private Libraries in Creole St. Louis. Baltimore, John Hopkins Press, 1938.
28. Jesse Shera, Foundations of the Public Library, op. cit., the best study for New England.
29. See Haynes McMullen, "The founding of Social Libraries in Pennsylvania, 1731-1876," Pennsylvania History 32:130-152, 1965.
30. See Ray E. Held, Public Libraries in California, 1849-1878. Berkeley, University of California Press, 1963.
31. See Haynes McMullen, "Social Libraries in Ante-Bellum Kentucky," The Register of the Kentucky Historical Society 58:97-128, 1960.
32. Anthony Thomas Kruzas, Business and Industrial Libraries in the United States, 1820-1940. New York, Special

Libraries Association, 1965.

33. Robert V. Williams, "Document Sources for the History of Federal Government Libraries," in John David Marshall (ed.) Approaches to Library History, op. cit., p. 61.

34. Edward Holley, "Neglect of the 'Greats,' Some Observations on the Problems of Writing the Biographies of American Librarians," Library Journal 88:3547, 1963.

35. Laurel Ann Grotzinger, The Power and the Dignity, Librarianship and Katharine Sharp. New York, Scarecrow Press, 1966.

36. The "Library Hall of Fame," Library Journal 76:466-472, 1951, offers a list of 40 leaders in the library movement; only a few have been the subjects of serious biographical research.

37. Robert B. Downs, "Resources for Research in Librarianship," Library Trends 13:8, 1964.

38. There is a history of the Special Library Association, but it is a simple chronicle rather than an assessment. See Alma Clarvoe Mitchill (ed.) Special Libraries Association - Its First Fifty Years, 1909-1959. New York, Special Libraries Association, 1959.

II

American Library History: Philosophy and Methodology
For Research

A Brief Guide to Books on the Methodology and Philosophy of History

A number of volumes offer the beginning historian an introduction to the whole field of historical research in a compact and readable package. The first chapters of the Harvard Guide to American History[1] concisely outline the philosophy, methodology, and means of presentation of research in American history. The bibliographies, although somewhat out of date, still serve as good guides to further reading.

The Modern Researcher by Barzun and Graff[2] presents a highly readable introduction to the process of historical research, from the first steps of investigation to the final preparation of the paper. Beginners will find Allan Nevins The Gateway to History[3] a provocative introduction to history as both art and science. Library historian Jesse Shera presents a brief but useful survey of historical research in his Historians, Books and Librarians. [4]

The philosophy of history is concisely treated by a number of recent books: W. H. Walsh, Philosophy of History: an Introduction[5] and William H. Dray, Philosophy of History[6] are both well written and offer extensive guides to further reading.

Two of the best introductions to the historical method are Homer Carey Hockett, The Critical Method in Historical Research and Writing[7] and Louis R. Gottschalk, Understanding History: A Primer of Historical Method. [8] Hockett's book is especially useful to American historians.

Because most research in American library history is concerned with individual libraries the researcher will find useful Donald D. Parker, Local History: How to Gather It, Write It, and Publish It[9] and Philip D. Jordan, The Nature and Practice of State and Local History. [10] Clarence E. Carter,

Historical Editing[11] will prove of service to researchers working with documents and letters.

Anyone considering biographical research can do no better than to read J. A. Garraty, The Nature of Biography,[12] which deals with the history, theory and practice of biography in an entertaining and enlightening manner.

The Value of American Library History

Unlike most historians, who are careful not to emphasize the utilitarian aspect of their work, many American library historians stress the value of library history in the practical administration of libraries. Pierce Butler illustrated this point of view when he stated, "Librarianship, as we know it, can be fully apprehended only through an understanding of its historic origins."[13] He pointed out that many current situations in individual libraries are "hopelessly puzzling" until one understands the history of the personal elements that have entered into their development.[14]

Stanley Pargellis applied this theory to book selection when he wrote, "Every librarian ought to fit, if he can, another stone into his own institution, another book. To do that intelligently he should know the policies his library has followed in the past..."[15] Haynes McMullen made the same point: "If we are to operate our libraries wisely in the present, we need to know how libraries have been operated in the past."[16] Shirley Dean Hake saw library history as an aid to future library planning: "The purpose of this study is to assist in the planning of library development for the future by an examination of factors which have hindered or promoted its growth in the past."[17]

Jesse Shera also saw an understanding of library history as vital for, as he indicated, there have been a number of points in American library history where "a disregard for library history has resulted in confused thinking and much misdirected effort, consequences which eventually are professionally disastrous and socially regrettable."[18] A number of other librarians have also found that a lack of historical perspective has proven costly in both time and money.[19]

The above quotations are not meant to imply that library historians envisage a strictly utilitarian application of library history, for they also stress the value of library history for developing the mind, deepening the sympathies, and breaking down the provincialism and specialization of so many

American librarians. [20] Nevertheless, there is a strong emphasis on the value an understanding of library history offers for the present and future administration of libraries.

Philosophy and Methodology in American Library History

The investigation and writing of American library history has tended to follow the paths traced by historians investigating other social institutions. The publication of Josiah Quincy, History of the Boston Athenaeum, in 1851 has been cited as the appearance of the first formal history of an American library. [21] From that time until the third decade of the twentieth century, most published library histories were antiquarian and sentimental in approach, rarely venturing beyond straight description.

In 1931 Arnold K. Borden, writing in the Library Quarterly, argued for a new approach to library history, which illustrated [see note 22] that "the new concepts of the social philosophers were beginning to percolate downward to the librarians' own little cosmos. "[22] Borden felt that library historians "must not look upon the library as an isolated phenomenon or as something which has been struck off the brains of individuals in moments of philanthropic zeal... From the point of view of history as well as contemporary conditions the library needs to be studied in the light of sociology, economics and other branches of knowledge. "[23]

Borden's essay, while not a definitive exposition of that new approach, was widely read. At least one noted American library historian acknowledged the strong impact the article made on his thinking. [24] Borden's article heralded what Shera has termed the "New Library History. "

This new approach emphasized the analysis and interpretation of library development in relation to the "complex of social ideas, conditions, and forces which led to its establishment and subsequently shaped its character. "[25] The acceptance of this philosophy and its later application gave rise in quick succession to a number of classic studies of American library history: Jesse Shera, Foundations of the Public Library, Sidney Ditzion, Arsenals of a Democratic Culture, and Gwladys Spencer, The Chicago Public Library. [26] Most library historians have since used this approach in their research. Unhappily, most have proven a good deal less successful than the above mentioned authors.

Attempts at outlining the methodology of research on

American library history have been few, for most library
historians now accept the above stated philosophy and apply
the historical method used by historians in general to their
research. The best guide to methodology in library history
is often an examination of the published histories.

The only lengthy exposition of the philosophy and
methodology of library history will be found in H. J. Vleeschauwer, Library History in Library Science. [27] Dr. Vleeschauwer, Professor of Library Science at the University of
South Africa, agreed with Borden's argument that the library
cannot be treated as an isolated phenomenon:

> No matter how highly one may value the cult-
> ural role of the library, it is and remains an
> auxiliary institution. Since it is always a part
> of a greater intellectual whole, the library
> exists to fulfill a function, which reaches much
> further than itself. The whole defines the na-
> ture and existence of the library: lends a sci-
> entific character to its expositions and lends
> tone to its historic approach. [28]

From this point of origin Professor Vleeschauwer discusses such subjects as the scientific value of library history;
the educational value of library history; the uses of library
history; the historic method and library history; "objective
impediments" of library history; "subjective impediments"
of library history; and the "true object" of library history.
In regard to the last point Vleeschauwer stresses the need
for analysis and interpretation. He argues that after we have
found "what has been" we must go on to find out "why." We
must "trace causes and deduce from the available data what
factors were responsible for certain developments."[29] Although broad in scope and difficult to read, this volume will
prove stimulating and enlightening to the researcher.

Several library historians have presented short outlines of the methodology for research in American library
history. Two papers in this area were presented at the Library History Seminar held at Florida State University in 1961.
Frank Sessa briefly listed the steps to be followed in research
in public library history, [30] while Willard D. Mischoff described the task of writing the history of academic (college and university) and school libraries. [31] Both papers described the
sources of information, the collection and analysis of data,
and the final presentation of the results.

21

An interesting research technique can be found in Haynes McMullen's report on his use of edge-notched cards in a study of nearly 7,000 American libraries established before 1876. [32]

Notes

1. New York, Atheneum, 1967.
2. New York, Harcourt, Brace, 1957.
3. Garden City, New York, Doubleday, 1962.
4. Cleveland, Western Reserve University Press, 1963.
5. New York, Harper and Row, 1960.
6. Englewood Cliffs, N. J., Prentice Hall, 1964.
7. New York, Macmillan, 1955.
8. New York, Alfred A. Knopf, 1950.
9. New York, Social Science Research Council, 1950.
10. Washington, Service Center for Teachers of History, 1958. Publication No. 14.
11. Washington, Government Printing Office, 1952. National Archives Bulletin No. 8.
12. New York, Vintage Books, 1957.
13. Pierce Butler, An Introduction to Library Science. Chicago, University of Chicago Press, 1964. p. 81.
14. Ibid, p. 82.
15. Stanley Pargellis, "Long Life to the Library History Round Table," in John David Marshall (ed.) American Library History Reader. Hamden, Conn., Shoestring Press, 1960. p. 8.
16. Haynes McMullen, "Why Read and Write Library History," Wilson Library Bulletin 26:385, 1952.
17. Shirley Dean Hake, A History of Library Development in Kittitas County, Washington (Unpublished master's thesis,) University of Washington, 1953. p. 3.
18. Jesse Shera, "On the Value of Library History," Library Quarterly 22:240-251, 1952.
19. See Robert Ellis Lee, Continuing Education for Adults Through The American Public Library, 1833-1964. Chicago, American Library Association, 1966. p. vi.
20. For other papers on the value of library history see Louis Shores, "The Importance of Library History," in John David Marshall (ed.) op. cit., p. 3-7, and R. Irwin, "Does Library History Matter," Library Review 128:510-513, 1958.
21. Jesse Shera, "The Literature of American Library History," Library Quarterly 15:1-24, 1945. This essay is the best history of the research and writing of American library history up to 1945.
22. Ibid., p. 18. See also Arnold K. Borden, "The Sociological

Beginnings of The Library Movement," _Library Quarterly_
1:278-282, 1931.
23. Borden, op. cit., p. 282.
24. Shera, "The Literature of American Library History,"
op. cit., p. 17.
25. Sidney Ditzion, _Arsenals of a Democratic Culture._ Chicago, American Library Association, 1947. p. ix.
26. Chicago, University of Chicago Press, 1943.
27. H. J. Vleeschauwer, "Library History in Library Science,"
Mousaion, Nos. 29 and 30, 1958. p. 87.
28. Ibid., p. 16.
29. Ibid., p. 72.
30. Frank Sessa, "Public Library History," in John David
Marshall (ed.) _In Pursuit of Library History._ Tallahassee,
Florida State University Library School, 1961. p. 19-22.
31. Willard O. Mischoff, "Academic and School Library History," in John David Marshall, Ibid., p. 23-32.
32. Haynes McMullen, "Through History with Punch and
Needle: Edge-Notched Cards for Data on Early American
Libraries," in John David Marshall (ed.) _Approaches to
Library History._ Tallahassee, _The Journal of Library
History,_ 1966. p. 81-90.

III

American Library History: A Guide to the Sources

This chapter provides an annotated list of indexes, bibliographies and guides to information on the literature and sources of American library history.

1. General Indexes to the Published Literature on American Library History

As a first step, the researcher in American library history will want to consult the following five indexes to the published literature of the field. Used individually, each is incomplete; but in aggregate they provide relatively comprehensive coverage.

Burton, Margaret and Vosburgh, Marion E. A Bibliography of Librarianship. London, The Library Association, 1934.
>This volume, worldwide in coverage, contains many items on American library history. The entries are briefly annotated and there is an author and subject index.

Cannons, H. G. T. Bibliography of Library Economy, 1876-1920. Chicago, The American Library Association, 1927.
>Indexes more than 60 British and American library periodicals and contains many items on American library history.

Library Literature, 1921-1932. New York, H. W. Wilson, 1934. Issued quarterly and cumulated annually.
>A basic indexing tool for the period from 1920 to date. It indexes library periodicals, books, and pamphlets, and is the most complete single indexing tool available.

Library Science Abstracts. London, The Library Association, 1950-. Issued quarterly, Cumulative Index to Volumes 1-6, 1950-1955. London, The Library Association, 1957.
>This publication indexes a number of items on American library history each year and should be used as a supplement to Library Literature.

Writings on American History, 1902, 1903, 1906-1940, 1948-. Princeton, New York, New Haven, and Washington, 1904-. 1941-1947 never issued. Latest volume to date is 1957.
>Each volume lists numberous articles and books on American library history under the heading "Libraries, Associations, and Institutions," of great importance since none

of the other indexes cover historical journals. A cumulated Index to the Writings on American History, 1902-1940, Washington, American Historical Association, 1956, saves time and effort when searching for specific subjects through 1940.

2. Critical and Descriptive Guides to American Library History

A number of bibliographic essays and descriptive bibliographies on American library history have appeared over the past thirty years. There is still much to be done, but the following items will prove useful to library historians.

Bach, Harry, Bibliographical Essay on the History of Scholarly Libraries in the United States, 1800 to the Present. University of Illinois Library School Occasional Papers, #54, Jan. 1959. 11 pp.

Since no one has attempted to prepare a critical bibliography of American library history, the researcher must turn to the bibliographies in specialized studies to locate the best sources of information on various phases of library development in the United States. This list of such sources is valuable for its evaluation of earlier studies that provide bibliographies and guides to materials of interest. Two other selective bibliographies should also be noted here. Articles on American Literature Appearing in Current Periodicals, 1920-1945, Durham, N. C., Duke University Press, 1947, edited by Lewis Leary, contains a carefully selected list of articles on colonial library history in the section entitled "Libraries and Reading." and V. A. Schaefer, A Contribution Toward a Bibliography of the Predecessors of the American Public Library (unpublished master's thesis), University of Michigan, 1933, is still useful.

Downs, Robert B., "Resources for Research in Librarianship," Library Trends 13:6-14, 1964.

This paper briefly describes some of the primary and secondary sources of information of use to the library historian, and indicates where they may be found.

Library of Congress, General Reference and Bibliography Division, A Guide to the Study of the United States of America. Washington, Government Printing Office, 1960.

This volume contains extensive descriptive annotations of a number of significant monographic studies on American library history, p. 1072-1080.

Mischoff, Willard O., "Academic and School Library History," in John David Marshall, (ed.) In Pursuit of Library History. Tallahassee, Florida State University Library School, 1961.

25

p. 23-32.

Mischoff discusses the difficulties facing the academic and school library historian, indicates the methodology and precautions the library historian should observe, and lists useful types of primary source material.

Mischoff, Willard O., "Sources for Library History," in John David Marshall (ed.) In Pursuit of Library History. Tallahassee, Florida State University Library School, 1961. p. 33-42.

Dr. Mischoff analyzes both published and manuscript sources of information of interest to the library historian, and indicates where they will be found and what role they should play in American library history. This paper complements his above mentioned paper.

Sessa, Frank B., "Public Library History," in John David Marshall (ed.) In Pursuit of Library History. Tallahasee, Florida State University Library School, 1961. p. 19-22.

Sessa briefly assesses the state of the art, describes the primary source materials of use to the public library historian, and offers some suggestions on the writing of library history. The public library historian will also want to see P. J. Bengtson, Bibliography of the Beginnings of Children's Library Work in the United States, 1876-1901. (unpublished master's thesis) Carnegie Institute of Technology, 1954.

Shera, Jesse H. "The Literature of American Library History," Library Quarterly 15:1-24, 1945.

In this essay Shera does three things: (1) he evaluates the literature of American library history from 1850 to the fourth decade of the 20th century; (2) he traces the development of the research and writing of American library history during the same period; and (3) he discusses the difficulties the library historian faces, pointing out what he feels are the most serious research needs in the field of American library history. The latter suggestions are still timely, and his reasoned evaluation of the literature remains the best commentary on American library histories published before 1945.

Stewart, Nathaniel, "Sources for the Study of American College Library History, 1800-1876," Library Quarterly 13:227-231. 1943.

Stewart describes the years between 1800 and 1876 as the most neglected period in American college library history. That statement remains true today. In this paper Stewart discusses the primary and secondary sources of information on the development of college libraries from 1800 to 1876, and describes various approaches that might be followed in writing about the history of these libraries.

Another bibliography that is still useful is Hugh Williams, College Libraries in the United States. Contribution Towards a Bibliography. Albany, University of the State of New York, State Library Bulletin--bib. #19--1899. p. 609-655. For information relating to college literary society libraries see Catherine P. Storie, What Contributions Did the American College Society Library Make to the College Library. (unpublished master's thesis) Columbia, 1938. Two especially useful chapters are "Sources for Locating College Society Libraries" p. 8-28, and "Sources for Locating Catalogs of College Society Libraries" p. 29-51.

Williams, Robert V., "Document Sources for the History of Federal Government Libraries," in John David Marshall (ed.) Approaches to Library History... Tallahassee, Florida State University Library, 1966. p. 61-80.

The first part of this paper is a discussion of ways to approach historical research on federal libraries, while the second part is a bibliography of primary and secondary sources of use in such research. The bibliography is extensive but not exhaustive and is intended to serve as a starting point in research on the history of federal libraries. It is divided into four parts: (1) Bibliographic Guides; (2) Best Sources for the History of Early Government Libraries; (3) General Sources for History of Government Libraries; and (4) Sources for Study of the History of Particular Federal Libraries.

Woods, Bill M., "Library Association Archives and Library History," in John David Marshall (ed.) Approaches to Library History... Tallahasee, Florida State University Library, 1966. p. 49-60.

In this paper Woods suggests ways to improve the archives programs of library associations, which generally are very poorly organized. He indicates the types of library association records that are of use to the library historian. Of special interest is the "Inventory of Library Association Archives" p. 59-60, which gives details on the location, contents, and use policies of the archives belonging to thirteen major American library associations.

3. Sources of Biographical Information on American Libraries

American librarians have seldom been the subjects of serious historical research. One can point to only six full-length scholarly biographies of American librarians. The long months of locating, gathering and interpreting data, and the equally long task of writing have discouraged many busy librarians from undertaking such a job. Thus published information on individual American librarians is scarce, and primary sources are even more difficult to locate. The following list, meager as it is, will provide some initial aid in gathering information of American librarians.

Indexes to Biographical Material

Biography Index. New York, H. W. Wilson, 1947-. Monthly; cumulated annually.
> This index, because of its wide scope, often includes materials on American librarians. An occupational index to each volume makes it easy to use. The first volume covers material published after January 1, 1946.

Library Literature. New York, H. W. Wilson, 1934-.
> Even very brief mentions of individual American librarians that appear in publications on library science are indexed in this tool.

Collections of Biographies

Danton, Emily Miller (ed.) Pioneering Leaders in Librarianship. Chicago, American Library Association, 1953.
> Presents brief biographies of eighteen library pioneers who lived between 1836-1944.

Dictionary of American Biography. New York, Scribner, 1928-1937, 20 v. Supplements 1-2. New York, Scribner, 1944-1958, 2 v.
> The only multi-volume biographical work that gives extensive coverage to leading American librarians. Seventy-four librarians are covered in the first twenty volumes (see Stanley Pargellis, "Long Life to the Library History Round Table" in John David Marshall (ed.) American Library History Reader, p. 14, footnote 3, for a list).

Marshall, John David (ed.) An American Library History Reader. Hamden, Conn., Shoestring Press, 1961.
> This volume, which contains the papers delivered before the American Library History Round Table, includes twenty-one biographical essays on American librarians. The papers vary in quality, but all of them offer a beginning for the prospective biographer.

Who's Who in Library Service: A Biographical Directory of Professional Librarians of the United States and Canada. 1st ed. New York, H. W. Wilson, 1933; 2nd ed. New York, H. W. Wilson, 1943; 3rd ed. New York, Grolier Society, 1955; 4th ed. Hamden, Conn., Shoestring Press, 1966.
> The brief biographies offered in these volumes are of use in establishing basic chronologies, education, positions, and achievements of American librarians.

Part Two

An Annotated Bibliography of Graduate Research
in American Library History
1908 Through 1965

Introduction to the Bibliography

Selection of Entries

A serious effort has been made to list every master's
thesis and doctoral dissertation on American library history,
including papers written for library science, history, English, and education departments. Most of these papers were
located through the following lists:

Graduate theses accepted by library schools in the United
States, Library Quarterly, 3:267-91 (July 1933); 4:639-41
(Oct. 1934); 6:74-83 (Jan. 1936); 9:193-203 (Apr. 1939);
17:43-57 (Jan. 1947); 20:289-99 (Oct. 1950); 21:290-97
(Oct. 1951); 22:36-37, 342-49 (Jan., Oct. 1952); 23:287-
95 (Oct. 1953); 24:392-400 (Oct. 1954); 25:386-96 (Oct.
1955); 26:367-74 (Oct. 1956); 27:327-34 (Oct. 1957); 29:
48-54, 256-64 (Jan., Oct. 1959); 30:274-79 (Oct. 1960);
32:62-70 (Jan. 1962); 33:334-49 (Oct. 1963); 34:387-95
(Oct. 1964) 36:38-48 (Jan. 1966).
Libraries. Master's Theses in Education, 1951/52-1965/66.
Cedar Falls, Iowa: Research Publications, 1953-1966.
Vol. 1-15.
Library Schools--Theses, 1936-(1965), Library Literature,
New York, Wilson, 1940-(1965).
Nathan M. Cohen, Barbara Denison, and Jessie C. Boeh-
lert. Library Science Dissertations; 1925-1960. An An-
notated Bibliography of Doctoral Studies. Washington,
Government Printing Office, 1963.

Entries

Bibliographical information for each entry is as follows: (1) author; (2) title; (3) school where the thesis or

dissertation was written; (4) date; (5) pages; and (6) bibliography, if any.

If the paper was published in a nearly complete form, this too is indicated. No effort has been made to list short periodical articles based on theses or dissertations.

Annotations

The annotations are descriptive; no effort at critical comment has been made. A number of papers, due to loss or use restrictions, were not available for examination.

Predecessors of the Public Library

Private Libraries and Reading Tasks

BAER, E A. Books, Newspapers, and Libraries in Pioneer St. Louis, (1808-1842). Master's thesis, University of Wisconsin, 1961. Not examined.   1

BRADLEY, Ruth. Books in the California Missions. Master's thesis, Columbia University, 1950. 42 pp., bibl. The author attempts to trace the history of the book collections located in California Catholic missions beginning in 1769. The study begins with a brief survey of a number of mission libraries in California in 1950, and then examines the historical references to books in the missions.   2

CANTRELL, Clyde Hull. The Reading Habits of Ante-Bellum Southerners. Doctoral dissertation, University of Illinois, 1960. 419 pp., bibl. This is a study of the reading of 13 ante-bellum Southerners from Alabama, Georgia, North and South Carolina, Virginia, Georgia and Mississippi. Primary sources of data were diaries, journals, autobiographies, and letters. The author found that contrary to the claims of many that southerners of this period were not well read, 1,157 titles were identified. Of these 741 were in the Humanities, 300 in the Social Sciences, 65 in the Sciences, and 51 miscellaneous. Dr. Cantrell found that few books by New England literary figures were read-- only about 11 percent of the total. This paper also includes representative lists of books advertised in contemporary southern papers.   3

CROOK, Miriam Russell. Collections of Books and the Beginnings of Libraries in the Oregon Territory from the Great Migration to the End of the Frontier Period.

Master's thesis, University of Washington, 1960. 174., bibl.
The study covers library history in the Oregon Territory
from 1842 to 1900 and describes the many types of libraries available on the frontier--circulating libraries, social
libraries, private libraries, religious and academic libraries, and the territorial libraries of Oregon and Washington. Brief histories of over 25 libraries are included. The
author found a wide assortment of materials available to
people from every walk of life, from the mountain man to
the university professor. The appendix contains numerous
catalogs of libraries in the Territory.   4

GOUDEAU, John Milford. Early Libraries in Louisiana: A
Study of Creole Influence. Doctoral dissertation, Western
Reserve, 1965. 2 V., bibl.
This study deals with the evolution of Creole culture and
its influence on library development in early Louisiana.
Six sections make up the work: (1) Historical and cultural
background; (2) Private libraries in New Orleans; (3) Plantation libraries; (4) Public and semi-public libraries; (5)
Booksellers and printers in New Orleans; and (6) Summary.
A good deal of the information on private libraries was
drawn from will inventories and a number of the more important lists are found in an appendix to Volume I. Volume
two is wholly devoted to a list of source materials.   5

HOULETTE, William D. Plantation and Parish Libraries in
the Old South. Doctoral dissertation, University of Iowa,
1933. Not examined.   6

KEYS, Thomas Edward. Private and Semi-Private Libraries
of the American Colonies. Master's thesis, University of
Chicago, 1934. 89 pp., bibl.
This study is based on an analysis of data relating to book
ownership found in early catalogs and inventories of early
libraries as recorded in wills. On the basis of his data
Mr. Keys concludes that in New England the best libraries
were owned by the clergy and government officials, while
Virginia's libraries were owned largely by the cavalier
planters. Mr. Keys notes the difference in reading interests between the two groups--the Virginia planter was
far more interested in secular reading than in the theological books favored in New England. Mr. Keys also presents ideas on specific reading interests of the day, based
on catalogs and will inventories.   7

MANNING, James W. Books in Early Oregon: 1821-1883. Master's thesis, University of Oregon, 1940. 187 pp., bibl.
The author finds that books were present in Oregon from
its first settlement by trappers and traders in the early
19th century. Books were difficult to come by and the settlers selected only those that might help them in their

31

frontier struggles--guidebooks, and books on medicine,
law, agriculture, and religion. Mr. Manning discusses the
private collections of early settlers, also the early subscription and church library collections. A separate chapter is devoted to the history of the Oregon State Library
from 1843 to 1883, and another deals with the Library Association of Portland.   8

WHEELER, Joseph T. Literary Culture in Colonial Maryland,
1700-1776. Doctoral Dissertation, Brown University, 1938.
Parts published in Maryland Historical Magazine, various
issues 1939-1943. Original dissertation not examined.
The published chapters deal with (1) Circulating libraries;
(2) Bray's Layman's Libraries and the Provincial Library;
(3) Private libraries in Maryland, 1700-1776; and (4) Book-
stores in Colonial Maryland.   9

Thomas Bray and American Libraries

GORDON, Norma S. Thomas Bray: A Study in Early Eighteenth-Century Librarianship. Master's thesis, Catholic University, 1961. 105 pp., bibl.
This paper, which examines Bray as a bookman extraordinary, attempts to determine the background and source
of his attitudes, the nature of his ideas on libraries and
books, his choice of books, and his ideas about their classification. It briefly assesses the influence of the Bray Libraries upon the American library movement. Appendices
include: (1) a general catalog for a provincial library (Boston); (2) secular works included in a parochial library sent
to Pamplico, New Jersey, in 1700; and (3) a catalog of a
typical layman's library.   10

LAUGHER, Charles Theodore. The Beginnings of the Library
in Colonial America: Dr. Thomas Bray and the Religious
Societies, 1695-1795. Doctoral dissertation, Western Reserve, 1963. 289 pp., bibl.
This is a history of the American libraries organized in
the 17th and 18th centuries by Thomas Bray, the Society
for the Propagation of the Gospel in Foreign Parts, and
Dr. Bray's associates. Bray was offered the Commissary
to Maryland in 1695, but refused unless he could win support for his plan to establish libraries in each of the parish-
es in Maryland. He soon realized that due to poor book
conditions generally, he would have to establish libraries
in all the colonies. Bray was responsible for the establishment of over 70 general, parochial, or layman's libraries.
Dr. Laugher finds Bray's ideas remarkably modern--he
planned for public support and protection, he foresaw a
subscription plan as the best method for making additions,

and he stressed the principle of free access. Bray's single
most significant contribution was the establishment of the
Society for the Propagation of the Gospel in 1701. This organization was extremely influential in the establishment of
colleges and libraries in America as well as in England. 11

MOLZ, Jean Barry. The Reverend Thomas Bray, Planner of
Libraries: A Study of an Early Benefactor of Maryland Libraries. Master's thesis, Drexel Institute of Technology,
1950. 41 pp., bibl.
The author traces the work of Bray in establishing in Maryland 29 parochial libraries for the clergy, one provincial
library and 11 lending libraries. These libraries, intended
for the religious instruction of the clergy and laity, lasted
only a few years after their founder's death in 1730. Three
reasons are cited for their failure: (1) the specialized nature of the collections was of little interest to most of the
colonists; (2) there was inadequate provision for continuing
and strengthening the collections; and (3) the people, as reflected by the attitudes of the legislature, had little interest
in supporting the libraries.   12

SAHLI, Marilyn Sue. Thomas Bray and the Founding of Libraries in Maryland. Master's thesis, Western Reserve,
1952. 35 pp., bibl.
This study traces the history of Thomas Bray's efforts to
establish libraries in Maryland after 1698 and evaluates
the success of the venture. Bray established nearly 30 libraries in Maryland, the largest one at Annapolis; the
smallest was in Talbot County and received only two books.
It is estimated that Bray sent over 34,000 books and tracts
to America. The author describes many of the collections
and indicates their use. He says the libraries failed for
two basic reasons: (1) little provision was made to found
new libraries, or to augment the collections after Bray's
death, and (2) the collections were forced on the colony
from without. They did provide excellent working collections for the Anglican clergy, and their existance prompted
the first American library law in South Carolina in 1700. 13

SEARCY, Herbert Lyman. Parochial Libraries in the American Colonies. Doctoral dissertation, University of Illinois,
1963. 234 pp., bibl. (D.A. 64-6146)
This study deals mainly with the library work of the Reverend Thomas Bray in the American colonies. Dr. Bray
was concerned about the lack of capable men to serve as
Anglican priests in the colonies. He felt that the establishment of libraries would help attract new recruits in addition to aiding the less qualified priests in their religious
duties. In the years 1695-1699, Bray met extensive difficulties, the most serious of which were financial, but he

persevered in his efforts until he had established nearly
40 parochial libraries containing nearly 35,000 items. Dr.
Bray envisioned his libraries as open to all readers, and
the books he chose were theological and practical in nature. Despite his efforts the libraries were not supported
by the local authorities and finally disappeared.   14

Social, Circulating, School District, and Sunday School Libraries.

BACKUS, Joyce. A History of the San Francisco Mercantile
Library Association. Master's thesis, University of California, 1931. 191 pp., bibl.
This study covers the history of the San Francisco Mercantile Library from its origination in 1853 to 1905, when
it was merged with the Mechanics Institute. Regrettably
the collections of both libraries were destroyed by fire in
1906, before they could be combined. Started by a group
of education-minded Californians, the Mercantile Library
reached its high point in 1876, when it was adding some
2,000 volumes a year and had an annual circulation of
80,000. Cramped quarters, the depression of the later
1870's, and competition from other libraries are some of
the reasons cited for the library's rapid decline after
1876.   15
BURKE, Betty Louise. The Devlopment of Libraries in
Guilford, Connecticut. Master's thesis, Southern Connecticut State College, 1959. 60 pp., bibl.
The author presents a brief history of Guilford and traces
the development of libraries there dating from 1737, when
the cities of Guilford, Killingworth, Saybrook and Lyme
pooled their book resources and started the Four-Town
Library, up to 1959. She then examines six basic factors
that seemed to influence library development in Guilford:
(1) the librarian concept; (2) the role of women; (3) changes
in financial conditions; (4) the importance of local history
materials; (5) concern with school libraries; and (6) changes
in book selection policy.   16
CARTER, Merle. The Young Men's Mercantile Library Association of Cincinnati. Master's thesis, Western Reserve,
1951. 71 pp., bibl.
When this paper was written the Young Men's Mercantile
Library Association was 115 years old, one of the few
mercantile libraries still in existence. The author first
surveys the history of the mercantile library movement in
America and then chronologically traces the library's history from its inception in 1835 to 1950. From an original
45 members and 700 books, it grew to over 800 members

and 20,000 volumes in 1944. Numerous gifts and a relatively steady membership have enabled the library to maintain its high standards.   17

DAVIS, Elizabeth Gould. John Bradford's Contributions to
Printing and Libraries in Lexington, Kentucky, 1787-1800.
Master's thesis, University of Kentucky, 1951. 89 pp.,
bibl.
The major portion of this paper deals with Bradford's efforts on behalf of publishing and education in Kentucky. A
final chapter deals with his significant contributions to libraries in Lexington. Under his leadership the Transylvania Seminary Library, established in 1784, gained considerable stature after nearly failing due to disinterest of
the original directors. Out of this library grew the library
of Transylvania University, which was for many years the
largest and most famous library in the West. Bradford
was also the initial force behind the establishment of the
Lexington Library in 1795, which was one of the earliest
social libraries in the western United States.   18

DAY, Nancy Jane. History and Administration of the Social
Library of Bedford, New Hampshire. Master's thesis,
University of Michigan, 1943. Not examined.   19

DODGE, Alice Cynthia. Origins of the School District Library
Movement in New York State. Master's thesis, University
of Chicago, 1944. 101 pp., bibl.
When the school district library law of 1835 was passed
in New York State, it incorporated the then forward-look-
ing principle of tax support. The author points out that
this principle had been previously endorsed by the Dutch
settlers in New York when they passed the 1812 education
act calling for community tax support. The movement gained impetus from this factor, plus (1) the new belief in
education (i.e., reading) as a safeguard of democracy; (2)
the example of already existing social libraries; and (3)
the influence of a number of public-spirited leaders. James
Wadsworth originated the idea of school district libraries,
Dr. Jesse Torrey, Jr., gave it support and a wide airing,
and Governor De Witt Clinton presented the idea to the
state legislature in 1825 and again in 1827. Once the libraries were established, most of them finally agreed on
buying books from a series of 295 titles known as the
Harper's School District Library. By 1850 there were nearly 1,500,000 volumes in the school district libraries of
New York.   20

FEDDER, Maxine Blanche. The Origin and Development of the
Sunday School Library in America. Master's thesis, Uni-
versity of Chicago, 1951. 139 pp., bibl.
The 19th century saw a rebirth of religious fervor and an

attempt at re-establishing the Church in America. The
author surveys the development of Sunday School libraries
during this period, with special emphasis on the influence
of the American Sunday School Union. Largely due to the
Union's efforts the Sunday School library was well established in America by 1830. By 1880 most protestant churches in America had a library; after this high point the Sunday School library met with a serious decline and by 1900
had faded from the picture. The author cites the following
causes of its demise: (1) the growth of children's reading
rooms in public libraries; (2) the poor administration of
Sunday School libraries; and (3) a growing trend toward the
secularization of Sunday School collections. Nevertheless,
the Sunday School library served an important intellectual
function during the half-century between 1830 and 1880. 21

FLENER, Jane Gardner. A History of Libraries in Tennessee
Before the Civil War. Doctoral dissertation, Indiana University, 1963. 169 pp. , bibl.
The author divides her paper into five major sections: (1)
a brief history of Tennessee before the Civil War; (2) a
history of over 25 social libraries in Tennessee before the
Civil War; (3) history of over a dozen college libraries in
Tennessee before 1860; (4) The Tennessee Historical Society Library and the Tennessee State Library; and (5) a
comparison of Tennessee libraries before the Civil War
with libraries in other states (Kentucky, South Carolina,
Ohio, Indiana, and Illinois). The author finds that for a
state that then had many sections not far removed from the
frontier stage of development, libraries had a firm footing.
Appendix A is a chronological list of social and special
libraries in Tennessee before the Civil War.   22

GRIMM, Dorothy Fear. A History of the Library Company of
Philadelphia, 1731-1835. Doctoral dissertation, University
of Pennsylvania, 1955. 367 pp. , bibl. (D. A. 55-1076)
Benjamin Franklin organized the first subscription library
in America in 1731, and the Library Company of Philadelphia proved more durable than any of its followers.
Nearly a thousand other subscription libraries rose and fell
during the period covered, but the Library Company of
Philadelphia endured through the revolution and numerous
other difficulties. Dr. Grimm points out how the development and evolution of the library closely paralleled the
history of the area. She discusses the development of the
library's collections, its extensive influence on Philadelphia,
and its evolution from a rather specific research library
to what approximated a public library.   23

HATCH, Orin Walker. Lyceum to Library: A Chapter in the
Cultural History of Houston. Master's thesis, University

of Houston, 1964. Published: Houston, Texas: Texas Gulf
Coast Historical Association, 1965. 73 pp., bibl.
Original thesis not examined. The published volume traces
the history of library development in Houston from 1837 to
1965. Most of the book is devoted to a history (1854-1904)
of the Houston Lyceum, out of which grew the Houston Pub-
lic Library.   24
KEEP, Austin B. The Library in Colonial New York. Doctoral
dissertation, Columbia University, 1909. Published: History
of the New York Society Library, with an Introductory
Chapter on Libraries in Colonial New York. New York, De-
vinne Press, 1908.
The published volume deals with the following subjects: (1)
Bray Foundation, Library at Trinity Parish; (2) the Sharpe
Collection; (3) the Corporation Library, 1730-1776; (4) New
York Society Library, 1754-1776; (5) Library of Kings Col-
lege, 1757-1776; (6) booksellers' circulating libraries,
1763-1776; and (7) the Union Library Society, 1771-1776. 25
MARTIN, Dorothy V. A History of the Library Movement in
Ohio to 1850 with a Special Study of Cincinnati's Library
Development. Master's thesis, Ohio State University, 1935.
83 pp., bibl.
The author traces library development in Ohio from its
earliest beginnings in the latter part of the 18th century
through 1950. This study is concerned mainly with social
libraries and deals with private collections only when they
evolved into social libraries. Library development in Cincinnati is described, beginning with the first efforts to
establish a social library in 1802 up through 1850. Appendices list the libraries incorporated by the Ohio legislature through 1850.   26
MOORE, Mary Virginia. Circulating Libraries in the Southeastern United States, 1762-1842: A Selected Study. Master's thesis, University of North Carolina, 1958. 84 pp.,
bibl.
After tracing the origins of the circulating library in England in the early 18th century, the author describes its
development in America. The major portion of the paper
is devoted to a history of circulating libraries in five major southeastern cities: Annapolis, Baltimore, Fredericks-
burg, Charleston, and Savannah. Most of the libraries were
established by businessmen, mainly stationers, booksellers,
and printers, and were aimed at attracting additional business to their stores. They proved to be relatively successful ventures but were nearly always subsidiary to the own-
ers' main business. The growing popularity of the novel
in America is cited as a major reason for the growth of
the circulating library, and the author links the circulating

library with the development of the public library.   27

O'CONNER, Sister Mary Victoria. History of the Redwood Library and Athenaeum of Newport, Rhode Island. Master's thesis, Catholic University, 1956. 74 pp., bibl.
This paper traces the history of the Redwood Library from 1747 to 1950. It was founded with a 500-pound donation from Abraham Redwood, followed by a gift from Henry Collins of a piece of property on which to erect a building. The author describes the economic difficulties the Redwood Library faced and the effect of the Revolutionary and Civil Wars on its development. After 1865, the library made consistent progress.   28

REILLY, Pamela G. Some Nineteenth-Century Predecessors of the Free Library of Philadelphia. Master's thesis, Drexel Institute of Technology, 1951. 53 pp., bibl.
After first describing library facilities in Philadelphia up to 1800, the author analyzes six libraries considered predecessors of the Free Library. They are the Athenaeum, the German Society Library, the Apprentices' Library, the Mercantile Library, the Library Company, and the Philadelphia City Institute Library. No attempt is made to give a thorough history of each library; the libraries are studied in terms of their services to the public of 19th-century Philadelphia. The aims of the libraries, their book collections, types of clientele, and special services are covered. This study goes to 1891, when the Free Library was established.   29

RICHIE, Joan Frances. Railroad Reading Rooms and Libraries in Ohio, 1865-1900. Master's thesis, Kent State, 1965. 86 pp., bibl. Published: ACRL Microcard #149.
Traces the development and expansion of Ohio's railroad reading rooms and libraries in the period from 1865 to 1900. The author discusses the origins, purposes, locations, longevity and services of the railroad reading rooms, with special attention to the efforts of the YMCA and the vigorous activities of temperance groups in Ohio from 1865-1900. The considerable influence of John Henry Devereaux, railroad executive and financier, on the development of railroad reading rooms and libraries in Ohio is also discussed.   30

ROBINSON, Ruth Willard. Four Community Subscription Libraries in Colonial Pennsylvania: Darby, Hatboro, Lancaster, and Newtown, 1743-1790. Doctoral dissertation, University of Pennsylvania, 1952. 291 pp., bibl. (D.A. 12, 159.)
Traces the history of the four community subscription libraries in 18th-century Pennsylvania from the establishment of the Darby Library Company in 1743 until 1790.

The author begins with a general discussion of the development of subscription libraries in America. She then examines in detail the colonial background of the four communities, with a consideration of the people and events influential in the founding of the libraries. The history of the four libraries is presented in chronological order: Darby, founded 1743; Union Library Company, founded 1755; Newtown Library Company, founded 1760; and Lancaster Library Company, founded 1759. The Lancaster Library Company was the only one not in existence in 1952. The author finds that literature was the most popular reading material in the four libraries, modifying the concept of the utilitarian reading interests of the colonials. Appendices contain copies of the catalogs of the books owned by each library up to 1790.   31

SABINE, Julia Elizabeth. Antecedents of the Newark Public Library. Doctoral dissertation, University of Chicago, 1946. 169 pp., bibl.
The author is concerned with the factors that led to the establishment of the Newark Public Library in 1888. She analyzes the social and intellectual background of the Middle Atlantic States, with emphasis on New Jersey. The influence of the Newark Library Association from 1845 to 1888 is carefully traced. The author finds the following factors influential in the founding of the Newark Public Library: (1) the precedent of subscription libraries; (2) the urge for self-improvement; (3) a demand for wholesome literature for young people; (4) enabling legislation; and (5) an expanding economy.   32

SHERA, Jesse H. Foundations of the Public Library: The Origins of the Public Library Movement in New England, 1629-1855. Doctoral dissertation, University of Chicago, 1944. 341 pp., bibl. Published: University of Chicago, 1949. Reprinted, Shoe String Press, 1965.
Traces the history of library development in New England up to the establishment of the Boston Public Library, and discusses the social, economic, and cultural factors that influenced this development. An extensive treatment is given to the development of social and circulating libraries in New England. A careful analysis is made of the causal factors responsible for public library development: (1) national and local pride; (2) historical scholarship and the urge for preservation; (3) increasing concern with vocational problems; and (4) the contribution of religion.   33

SPAIN, Frances Lander. Libraries of South Carolina: Their Origins and Early History, 1700-1830. Doctoral dissertation, University of Chicago, 1944. 179 pp., bibl.
The author traces library development in South Carolina

from 1700, when the State legislature passed its first library law, to 1830. The library societies of Charleston (1748), Georgetown (1800), and Beaufort (c. 1802) are among those extensively discussed. The author finds that these libraries served only limited groups; that they were established only in stable urbanized areas with refined societies and ample economic resources; and that there was a very close relationship between church, school, and library. An appendix includes a chronological table of library societies in South Carolina from 1700 to 1837.   34

STIFFLER, Stuart A. The Antecedents of the Public Library in the Western Reserve, 1800-1860. Master's thesis, Western Reserve, 1957. 53 pp. , bibl.
The author surveys library development in the Reserve in terms of the socio-economic environment and popular beliefs of the 19th century, and their expression in reading and other literary activities. The first Cleveland library was organized in 1811, when 17 of the 45 residents of that city established a Library Association, and after that time many libraries rose and fell in the Reserve. The lack of organization structure, the increasing democratization of the social order, and recurrent financial crises are cited as factors in the demise of the social library. Appendix I is a list of libraries organized and incorporated in the Western Reserve, 1819-1850.   35

VAN BEYNUM, William J. United to Buy Books, a History of the Book-Company of Durham; A Public Library 1733-1865. Master's thesis, Southern Connecticut State College, 1961. 79 pp. , bibl.
Founded on the 30th of October, 1733, the Book-Company of Durham is generally recognized as the first proprietary library established in New England. The author is unable to ascertain exactly what inspired the founding of the library, whether Franklin's example was responsible, whether an English model provided an influence, or whether it was simply a spontaneous growth. The author assesses the value of the library in the education climate of the community, and then discusses the book purchases made by the library over the 123 years of its existence. Catalogs of the library's holdings and the articles of the Book-Company are included in the Appendix. The author also includes a list of books sent by the Rev. Thomas Bray to the Rev. Ichabod Camp of Middleton, New England.   36

WELBORN, Elizabeth Charles. The Development of Libraries in South Carolina, 1830-1860. Master's thesis, George Peabody College, 1956. 163 pp. , bibl.
This study encompasses all types of libraries, both social and academic. The author devotes about one third of her

paper to a history of libraries in Charleston, and then presents brief histories of some 30 libraries established outside of Charleston from 1830 to 1860. The author finds that the great majority of the 36 libraries in existence between 1830 and 1860 were social libraries. The next largest group were the academic libraries. The largest collection in the state in 1860 was that of the legislative library, with 25,000 volumes. Appendices include a "Chronological Table of Library Societies in South Carolina, 1700-1837"; and "Libraries Founded Between 1830-1860."   37

WILCOX, Helen Merrill. School District Public Libraries - A Step in Popular Education in the Nineteenth Century with Emphasis on the Period from 1820-1850. Master's thesis, Drexel Institute of Technology, 1953. 56 pp., bibl.
The author divides her paper in five major sections. First she sets the stage by describing the cultural, economic, and social conditions of the period covered. Second, she traces the development of the publishing industry from 1820 to 1850. Third, she presents a description of libraries already existing at that time. Fourth is an analysis of the origin and evolution of school district libraries from 1820 to 1850. And finally, the author analyzes the success and final demise of the school district libraries. The author finds that the school district libraries were forced upon the populace, rather than being a response to public demand. The founders of the systems were men of vision, and certainly the libraries served as a bridge between the old social library and the new public library. They failed for several reasons: (1) the governmental unit was too small (over 11,000 districts in New York); (2) there was a distinct lack of sound administration; and (3) the financial base was too small. Harper's School District Libraries Catalog, 1853, is included as an Appendix.   38

Public Libraries

General Studies

ANDERS, Mary Edna. The Development of Public Library Services in the Southeastern States, 1895-1950. Doctoral dissertation, Columbia University, 1958.   290 pp., bibl. (D. A. 58-2670)
The public library movement was slow in developing in the southeastern states. It was not until the last decade of the 19th century that any significant progress was made. During this period, the interest of women's clubs and professional leaders, along with generous Carnegie grants, led to the establishment of numerous free libraries in the

Southeast. Dr. Anders finds that the Southeast adopted
county and regional libraries more readily than did the
rest of the nation, and that the greatest growth in library
facilities took place after 1935. Financial capability was
found to be the overriding factor in library development in
the area.   39

ATKINS, Eliza. The Government and Administration of Public
Library Service to Negroes in the South. Doctoral dissertation, University of Chicago, 1940. 173 pp., bibl.
This study is primarily concerned with an appraisal (1940)
of the Southern Negro in relation to public libraries. However the author does trace in the introductory section the
history of library service to Negroes in the South. Almost
no service was offered before 1900. After that time the
Negro was given limited privileges at the main library or
else a special Negro branch library was established. Louisville, Kentucky, was a leader in early attempts at providing extensive service to Negro patrons.   40

BELL, Bernice Lloyd. Integration in Public Library Service
in Thirteen Southern States, 1954-1962. Master's thesis,
Atlanta University, 1963. 134 pp., bibl.
Although this paper concerns itself mainly with the present
status (1962) of library service to Negroes in the South, it
also presents brief digests of the historical development of
this service in the following states: Alabama, Arkansas,
Florida, Georgia, Kentucky, Louisiana, Mississippi, North
and South Carolina, Oklahoma, Tennessee, Texas and Virginia.   41

CARRIER, Esther Jane. Fiction in Public Libraries of the
United States, 1896-1900. Doctoral dissertation, University
of Michigan, 1960. 592 pp., bibl. Published: Scarecrow
Press, 1965.
The author presents an analysis of the philosophy and
policies American librarians and public libraries held regarding fiction during the last quarter of the 19th century.
Through the use of materials from the Library Journal
and Public Libraries, plus contemporary reviews from a
number of other magazines, the author is able to isolate
points of contention and agreement. Dr. Carrier finds
that no solution to the problem of fiction's place in the
public library was arrived at during the period covered.
Two points were generally agreed on, that no immoral
books should be presented and that libraries should make
a serious attempt to raise the level of reading sophistication.   42

CLOPINE, John Jr. A History of Library Unions in the United
States. Master's thesis, Catholic University, 1951. 183 pp.,
tables, bibl. Published: ACRL Microcard #43.

Studies the history of library unions in the United States
from the establishment of the first union in the Library
of Congress in 1916 up to 1955. The author finds that
library unions have existed only in limited geographical
areas. No locals had appeared in the far West by 1955,
while only one local (Atlanta) had appeared in the South.
Most unions were established in the Great Lakes or Middle Atlantic states areas, and all but three of the unions
developed in cities of 250,000 or more residents. The
mortality rate among library unions was found to be very
high.   43

COLLIER, Francis G. A History of the American Public Library Movement Through 1880. Doctoral dissertation, Harvard, 1953.

Traces public library history from the social library to
state, county and school district libraries and finally to
the local tax-supported public library. By 1880 over 200
public libraries had been established; Massachusetts had
the largest number, followed by Illinois and Ohio. The
author discusses the influence of three events in 1876:
the founding of A.L.A.; the founding of the American Library Journal; and the publication of the influential report
Public Libraries in the United States of America: Their
History, Conditions and Management.   44

DAVIS, Faye C. The Development of the Traveling Library.
Master's thesis, East Texas State College, 1959. 68 pp.,
bibl.

The author devotes about a third of his paper to a survey
of the history of the traveling libraries, from their beginnings in Scotland in 1730 up to 1959. As early as 1831,
under the stimulus of the lyceum movement, the first
"itinerating libraries" were proposed. These were followed by libraries housed on American ships, in hospitals and
in lighthouses. In 1892 the first general American traveling libraries supported by public funds were authorized by
the New York State Legislature. In subsequent years every
state instituted traveling library systems. The 20th century proved a turning point in the development of the traveling library. Federal support, through such programs as
the Civilian Conservation Corps, the Works Progress Administration, and the Library Services Act, was a major
factor in this development. This commitment and the ever-
increasing use of bookmobiles have made traveling collections a highly significant part of the American library picture.   45

DITZION, Sidney H. Arsenals of a Democratic Culture: A Social History of the American Public Library Movement in
New England and the Middle Atlantic States from 1850 to

1900. Doctoral dissertation, Columbia University, 1945.
Published: A. L. A., 1947.

Traces the growth of the public library in the East in relation to social, economic and political factors. Dr. Ditzion discusses the transition from social library pioneers, the influence of ideas such as democracy and humanitarianism, philanthropy, and the services offered by early public libraries. [46]

DITZION, Sidney. The Public Library Movement in the United States as It Was Influenced by the Needs of the Wage Earner; 1850-1900. Master's thesis, College of the City of New York, 1938. 155 pp., bibl.

The author discusses, from the point of view of educational, economic and humanitarian purpose, the development of public library services to readers of all kinds, with special emphasis on the wage earner. He begins with an examination of the predecessors of the tax-supported free library, and follows with a discussion of the origins of, and justifications for, the tax-supported library. Finally he considers the expansion of public library services as they related to the wage earners' interests. Dr. Ditzion concludes that five factors were major influences in the development of the public library: philanthropy; the labor movement; the organized library profession; the expansion of the educational system resulting in an increased demand for books; and humanitarianism. [47]

EBERHART, Lyle. Concepts of the (American) Library's Role in Adult Education, 1926-1951. Master's thesis, University of Wisconsin, 1951. 45 pp., bibl.

This paper is a description of the evolution of an official philosophy and program in the area of library adult education over a 25-year period. The author finds that the 20's gave birth to three basic functions of adult education in the library: to render direct service to individuals; to act as a clearing house for community adult education activities; and to serve as the library for organized adult education classes. Despite this threefold purpose, the emphasis was on planned reading courses guided by readers' advisors. During the war years, librarians evidenced a new idealism in relation to adult education, a feeling that the public library could take the lead in guarding America's freedom. After the war this philosophy changed. More emphasis was placed on having the whole professional staff play a role in adult education, on working with groups, and on the use of audio-visual materials. [48]

HERDMAN, Margaret M. The Public Library in Depression. Doctoral dissertation, University of Chicago, 1941. 116 pp., bibl.

This study, covering the period 1930-1935, provides a picture of how the public libraries weathered a great economic depression. Based on statistics gathered from some 150 American public libraries, this study points out the courses of action taken by libraries when they had to cut back their budgets in the face of increased work loads.   49

KLOPENSTEIN, Martha Jane. The American Library and Some of Its Benefactors. Master's thesis, Western Reserve, 1955. 83 pp., bibl.

The author examines the factors that stimulated men to give money for the establishment of libraries in America. Twenty philanthropists are discussed and motives such as patriotism, local pride, practicality, genuine interest, egotism, charity, religion, democracy, and humanitarianism are delineated. The study is chronological and deals with the following men: Robert Keayne, Ben Franklin, John Jacob Astor, Henry Barnard, Joshua Bates, Edward Everett, Abbott Lawrence, George Peabody, George Ticknor, Francis Wayland, Daniel Fiske, James Lenox, Enoch Pratt, John Crerar, Walter Newberry, Andrew Carnegie, John D. Rockefeller, John Sterling, and Henry Folger.   50

LEE, Robert Ellis. The Educational Commitment of the American Public Library: 1833-1956. Doctoral dissertation, University of Chicago, 1963. Published: A.L.A., 1966.

Original dissertation not examined. In the published volume Dr. Lee describes the "evolution of the adult education commitment of the American public library, with particular attention to the most prevalent interpretation of the library's educational services provided in each period discussed." (Preface)   51

MONROE, Margaret E. Evolving Conception of Adult Education in Three Public Libraries: 1920-1955. 539 pp., bibl. Published: Scarecrow Press, 1963.

After tracing the general history of adult education in American libraries 1920-1950, the author presents a historical analysis of the development of adult education activities in three particular libraries: the Kern County Free Library; the Enoch Pratt Free Library, and the New York Public Library, Circulation Department.   52

NOURSE, Louis M. A Comparison of the Establishment and Growth of County Libraries in California and New Jersey As Influenced by Their Respective Legal, Geographical, and Administrative Differences. Master's thesis, Columbia University, 1931. 110 pp., bibl.

Studies factors in the development of the individual features of each system. The development of California's county library system is traced from the establishment of the State Library in 1850, while New Jersey's system is discussed

from the founding of the New Jersey Library Commission
in 1900. The author finds that in both states one or two
individuals were responsible for the successful introduction of the county library system. In both systems there
was a great variation between state and county laws.   53

PURDY, Betsy A. Famous Children's Libraries; A Survey of
Five Libraries Devoted Exclusively to Work with Children.
Master's thesis, Pratt Institute, 1952. 51 pp., bibl.
This is a history and survey of five children's libraries,
only three of which are American--the Brownsville Children's Library, a branch of the Brooklyn Public Library;
the Fitchburg Youth Library of Fitchburg, Massachusetts;
and the Robert Bacon Memorial Library of Westbury, Long
Island, New York.   54

SLOAN, Roberta Murphy. The History of the Phonograph
Record in the American Public Library, Its Origins and
Growth Through 1949. Master's thesis, Western Reserve,
1950. 53 pp., bibl.
The author has divided her study into four parts: (1) a
survey of phonograph record history; (2) a short history
of the development of music collections in the public library; (3) an analysis of the forces that brought the record
into the library--such as women's clubs, music groups
and school teachers; and (4) a history of the phonograph
record in libraries as illustrated by early record collections and their growth to 1949, followed by a summation
of discernible trends.   55

SPEIRS, Charles H. The Effects of Political Censorship in the
United States on Public Libraries and Librarians from
1945 to 1955. Master's thesis, Western Reserve, 1957.
55 pp., bibl.
This study describes a crucial period in American library
history--the postwar years when the library faced a serious
attack of political censorship. After the end of World War
II, when the United States entered into a cold war with the
Communist bloc, the threat of subversion became upper-
most in the American mind. Groups throughout the United
States began to campaign to remove and exclude all material that might be considered anti-American from public
and school libraries. The author discusses those attempts
and shows how librarians and organizations tried to deal
with the situation.   56

STIBITZ, Mildred T. Relation of the Public Library to Workers Education, 1918 to 1939. Master's thesis, Columbia
University, 1949. 142 pp., bibl.
The author selected the period between the first and the
second World Wars because that was the time when workers education expanded rapidly and won the attention of

adult educators and librarians. The major themes presented
are (1) the extent to which libraries attempted to serve the
special needs of labor unions and workers' education classes; and (2) the specific programs and procedures developed
by libraries to implement these services.

Local Studies Arranged by State

Alabama

FONVILLE, Emma Ruth. A History of Public Library Service
to Negroes in Bessemer, Alabama. Master's thesis, Atlanta
University, 1962. 47 pp., bibl.
This paper presents a history of the development of library
services to Negroes in Bessemer, Alabama, from its beginnings in 1950 to 1962. The author emphasizes the legal
provisions for library service to Negroes. The Bessemer
Public Library was established in 1907, but it was not until
1950 that service was extended to Negroes, and then only
in a token fashion. In 1961 the Negro branch had only
3,774 volumes and was open only 20 hours per week. There
were 18,982 Negroes living in Bessemer at that time. 58
GRAYSON, Bessie Rivers. The History of Public Library Service for Negroes in Montgomery, Alabama. Master's thesis,
Atlanta University, 1965. 54 pp., bibl.
The first library in Montgomery was founded in 1899. It
evolved into a public library that until 1948 served only the
white population of the city. The first formal library service for Negroes was provided in 1942 by the Rev. Ralph
O. Daly, a Negro, who set up a very limited service in
his church. This small library grew slowly into the Union
Street Branch Library of the Montgomery Public Library,
and it served the Negro population of Montgomery until
1960. In 1960 the collection contained 4,000 books and the
number of registered borrowers numbered 4,283. In 1962
the Mongomery Public Library System was forced to inte-
grate by a court order. 59

Alaska

MAUSETH, Barbara Joanne. A Brief History of the Ketchiken,
Alaska Public Library, 1901-1956. Master's thesis, Univer-
sity of Washington, 1956. 34 pp. Not examined. 60
PHELPS, Dorothy Jane. Organization and Development of the
Alaska Department of Library Service, 1955-1959. Master's
thesis, University of Utah, 1960. 191 pp., bibl.
This paper deals with four major problems: (1) a history
of the libraries and library services before the organization

of the Department of Library Service in Territorial Alaska in 1955; (2) an analysis of the Department of Library Services under the new department to 1959; (3) a brief history of each of 32 public libraries in Alaska 1929-1959; and (4) a description of the effects of Public Law 597, Library Services Act of 1956, on public library development in Alaska. The author was the first head of the Department of Library Service.   61

STEWART, Jeannette. Library Service in Alaska; A Historical Study. Master's thesis, University of Washington, 1957. 141 pp., bibl.

Presents an outline of library service in Alaska from the days of Russian occupation up to 1957. The history of libraries in Alaska from 1900-1957 is described in terms of the type of library: territorial; community; college and university; school; government and special. The author finds that though libraries are considered an urban phenomenon, even in Alaska, where few large urban centers exist, libraries were established and withstood long periods of economic instability. The organization of the Department of Library Services (1955) is seen as a vital development in an area that has suffered from a lack of professional guidance.   62

Arkansas

GATES, Joan Kay. Library Progress in Tax-Supported Institutions in Arkansas, 1924-1949. Master's thesis, Catholic University of America, 1951. 65 pp., bibl.

This study traces the history of tax-supported libraries in Arkansas from 1924, when the first free library service began, to 1949. The author uses a number of statistical tables to illustrate this development. Four major sections deal with the state library system, city and community libraries, public school libraries, and college and university libraries. The author finds that all phases of library development for the 25 years covered lagged behind average development in the rest of the nation.   63

McNEIL, Gladys. History of the Library in Arkansas. Master's thesis, University of Mississippi, 1957. 60 pp., bibl.

This paper traces the history of Arkansas libraries from the establishment of William Woodruff's lending library in Little Rock in 1843 up to 1957. The first library law in Arkansas was passed in 1901, and in 1927 a county library bill was passed. The author lists and briefly describes the 19 county libraries established in Arkansas by 1941. The development of the State Library and the contents of the collections of various Arkansas libraries are treated.

A Directory of County and Regional Libraries lists the date each was organized, its location, and how it is supported, and the author appends a "Chronology of Library Work in Arkansas."

Colorado

MINNICK, Nelle Frances. A Cultural History of Central City, Colorado, from 1859 to 1880, in Terms of Books and Libraries. Master's thesis, University of Chicago, 1946. 121 pp., bibl.
Central City was settled in 1859, during the gold rush, and developed rapidly until 1879, when the discovery of silver in Leadville drew people away. The author outlines the social, economic and political nature of the times and then traces the history of local library movements. She also provides an analysis of local reading interests, based mainly on the Catalogue of the Public Library of Central City (1878). This catalog in full is provided as an appendix, while one of the tables (p. 63) is a list of 51 leaders of library movements in Central City 1860-1880, classified by occupation.   65

Connecticut

BRYAN, Barbara Day. Fairfield Public Library; Antecedents and Development. Master's thesis, Southern Connecticut State College, 1964. 115 pp., bibl.
The Fairfield Memorial Library had been preceded by at least eight local social libraries when it was founded in 1876 as an incorporated subscription library. In 1898 it was opened to the public on a no-fee basis, supported mainly by private funds. In 1950 it was renamed the Fairfield Public Library and became a city-supported agency. The author states that after World War II, the old library, with an increasing population to serve and faced with changing concepts of library service, was not able to meet reader needs and so was reorganized as a publicly supported library.   66
GATES, Elizabeth S. The Library-School Council of Wethersfield, Connecticut. Master's thesis, Southern Connecticut State College, 1964. 87 pp., bibl.
The first 20 pages of this paper are devoted to a survey of library development in Wethersfield from 1783, when the first subscription library was established, to 1960. All types of libraries are treated in this section--private, school, public, and academic.   67
GIDDINGS, Ruth L. The West Hartford Public Library: Its

History, Development and Present Status. Master's thesis, Southern Connecticut State College, 1965. 172 pp., bibl. The author had three objectives in mind when she wrote this paper: (1) to assemble, organize, and preserve a record of the history of the West Hartford Public Library; (2) to analyze different phases of the library's development in terms of the institutional patterns revealed in comprehensive studies of the public library movement; and (3) to analyze present conditions and recommend a future direction of service. The history of the West Hartford Public Library is traced, beginning with its early forerunners--the Western Division Book Society (1753), the West Hartford Library Association (1837), and the Free Circulating Library of the First Congregational Church (1883). The Library's history is analyzed in an effort to determine the ways in which it followed, or failed to follow, the institutional trends and patterns described in published studies of library development in New England.   68

LOWREY, Silvia Gerard Roberts. A History of Libraries in Madison (East Guilford), Connecticut. Master's thesis, Southern Connecticut State College, 1963. 201 pp., bibl. This paper treats the history of the libraries in the town of Madison, Connecticut, beginning from the time that Madison was still part of Guilford and continuing to 1963. The libraries discussed are the Four-Town Library serving colonial Lime, Saybrook, Killingworth and Guilford from 1737-1787; the Farmers Library serving East Guilford, and later Madison, from 1793 to about 1852; the People's Library serving Madison from 1852 to approximately 1857; the North Bristol Library in Madison in 1824; the East River Library Company, in existence from 1874 to the 1930's; and the Madison Library Association Library, which served Madison from 1878 until it was merged with the E. C. Scranton Memorial Library, which serves the town to this very day. The catalogs of several of these libraries appear in full in the appendices.   69

WAGGONER, Lois Breyer. The Development of the Cheshire Public Library. Master's thesis, Southern Connecticut State College, 1965. 128 pp., bibl. The author briefly discusses the antecedents of the Cheshire Public Library, and then describes its development from 1892 to 1965. In 1894 the town received a gift from Mrs. Julia Tompkins, and the Library Association of Cheshire was founded that same year. In 1903 subscription fees were abolished and the library became free to all residents of the city. The library developed very slowly until after World War II due to lack of financial support. The greatest growth has taken place since 1957.   70

RICHARDS, Emma S. Fifty Years with the Library Commission for the State of Delaware. Master's thesis, Drexel
Institute of Technology, 1951. 39 pp., bibl.
In 1951 the Library Commission of Delaware completed
its 50th year. The Library Commission, which now serves
only Kent and Sussex counties, formerly included New
Castle County as well. It was urged into existence by some
Delaware women's clubs that wanted to institute traveling
libraries in the state. The author discusses the Commission's role in circulating books through traveling libraries
and later bookmobiles, and assesses its influence on public
library development in the state.   71

District of Columbia

COOK, Verla R. A History and Evaluation of the Music Division of the District of Columbia Public Library. Master's thesis, Catholic University of America, 1952, 87 pp.,
bibl.
This paper begins with a brief history of music departments in public libraries in the United States and goes on
to trace the origins of the Music Division of the District
of Columbia Public Library. A final section is devoted to
a topical history of the various departments, i.e. cataloging, staff, quarters. In 1933 the Civic Works Administration assigned two people to prepare the collection for public
use. In 1934 a plea for financial aid from private sources
to open the collection to the public was successful and the
Division became a reality. Starting with a small collection of sheet music, the Division's holdings had grown to
over 15,000 compositions by 1951.   72
KING, Margaret L. Beginnings and Early History of the Public Library of the District of Columbia, 1896-1904. Master's thesis, Catholic University, 1953. 86 pp., bibl.
The author briefly discusses the predecessors of the Public Library of the District of Columbia, from the founding
of the District in 1800 to the establishment of the Public
Library in 1896. She then traces the history of the Public
Library up to the retirement in 1904 of its first administrator, Weston Flint.   73
MAPLES, Houston L. The Peabody Library of Georgetown,
District of Columbia; A History and Evaluation. Master's
thesis, Drexel Institute of Technology, 1952. 84 pp., bibl.
Presents a history of the Peabody Library of Georgetown
from its inception in 1876 as a privately endowed library
until 1935, when it was disbanded. The author illustrates

both the limitations and advantages of a library function-
ing without public funds, and evaluates the library's per-
formance over the 60-year period covered.   74

Florida

GILL, Sylvia. The History of the Miami Public Library
System, Miami, Florida. Master's thesis, Western Reserve, 1954. 131 pp., bibl.
As did many cities across America, Miami got its first
library service through the efforts of a women's club organized in 1900. In 1902 the club voted to circulate its
books for $1.50 per year to non-members. In 1912 rail-
road magnate Henry M. Flagler donated a parcel of land
worth around $20,000, so that the women's club could
build a meeting house and library. In 1923, due to the
land boom, the women were able to sell their $13,000
building and the property for nearly $400,000, which was
promptly spent on a beautiful new home for the club and
library. In 1924 the city began supporting the library,
and in 1936 a central library was established to serve
the entire city. The author traces the development of the
main library to 1950 and then devotes the second half of
the paper to brief histories of the branch libraries in
Miami.   75
THOMAS, Evelyn F. The Origin and Development of the Society of the Four Arts Library, Palm Beach, Florida.
Master's thesis, Florida State, 1958. 55 pp., bibl.
This study traces the evolution of the Library of the Society of the Four Arts, a social library, from its beginnings in 1940 to 1957. The paper is divided into three
parts: a description of the character of Palm Beach; a
history of the library's development; and an analysis of
the library's status in 1957. In 1940 the library was little
more than a collection of books, but by 1957 it had grown
to a good size, with a children's room, listening rooms,
and other physical improvements. The clientele was originally a selected group, but in 1957 the library was
opened to all on payment of an annual fee. The collection
has always stressed the fine and decorative arts, but has
developed other areas as well.   76

Georgia

ADKINS, B. M. History of Public Library Service to Negroes
in Atlanta, Georgia. Master's thesis, Atlanta University,
1951. 44 pp. Not examined.   77
CRITTENDEN, Juanita Louise Jones. A History of Public

Library Service to Negroes in Columbus, Georgia, 1831-1959. Master's thesis, Atlanta University, 1960. 43 pp., bibl.

When the new library of Columbus, Georgia opened in 1907 it was closed to Negroes. In 1950 it was still closed to Negroes. Back in 1938 the W. P. A. had instituted a summer reading program open to both races. By 1944 the Negro population was allowed to use the Spencer High School Library and in 1945 a small Negro branch library was established. This small library proved totally inadequate and in 1952 a new $70,000 Negro branch library was opened. By 1959 this collection contained only 15,000 volumes and had little success in acquiring books from the main library for the use of Negro patrons. In 1959 the librarian had no formal book budget. The author found that the Negroes, who made up 32.2 percent of the population of Columbus, were receiving an infinitesimal amount of the main library's total services.   78

HUTZLER, Helen C. History of the Rome, Georgia, Carnegie Library (1911-1961). Master's thesis, Catholic University, 1963. 108 pp., bibl.

Presents a chronological history of library development in Rome, Georgia, from the establishment of the first subscription library in 1879 to 1961. In 1911 the town received a Carnegie grant to build a public library building, but the library grew slowly until 1929 due to a lack of funds. In the 30's extensive W. P. A. help enabled the library to extend its hours, services and book collection. By 1962 the library was circulating 200,000 volumes per year. The library was integrated in 1963.   79

HOWARD, Lucille. The Statesboro Regional Library: History, Development and Services. Master's thesis, Florida State, 1964. 63 pp., bibl.

The author devotes about one third of this paper to a historical consideration of the Statesboro, Georgia Regional Library. Agitation for the establishment of regional libraries, which are economical and efficient, first began in 1922. In 1935 the State of Georgia found that over 70 percent of its population was without library service. This led to the establishment of a number of regional libraries, the first of which was in Athens. The Statesboro Regional Library, the third founded in Georgia, began operation in 1944. The author traces the antecedents of the system and its growth up to 1954.   80

REDD, Gwendolyn Lewis. A History of Public Library Service to Negroes in Macon, Georgia. Master's thesis, Atlanta University, 1961. 50 pp., bibl.

Traces the history of the community, and then presents

53

a history of library service to Negroes in Macon from 1928 to 1960. The first library service to Negroes was provided by a Negro branch established in 1928. Services, facilities, and the collections were very weak and in 1949 the library was discontinued. It was reopened in 1953 in a permanent location as the Amelia Hutchings Memorial Library. The author describes the development of this library to 1960, including the organization, staff, services, collection and physical plant. 81

Illinois

BERG, V. A. History of the Urbana Free Library, 1870-1894. Master's thesis, University of Illinois, 1948. 82 pp., bibl. Not examined. 82

BULLOCK, Esther U. A History of the Geneva Public Library. Master's thesis , Northern Illinois University, 1965. 110 pp., bibl.
The first attempt at establishing a public library in Geneva was made in 1874, but due to a lack of funds it quickly failed. Started again in 1894 with about 800 books, the library soon became too large for its rented quarters. However, it was not until 1908 that a new building, financed by a $7,500 grant from Andrew Carnegie, was finished. The first children's room was established in 1938 and the first professional librarian, Miss Ruth Sibley, was hired in 1953. As far back as 1897 the library had instituted a loan service to the prisoners in the county jail; over the years it has served schools, businesses and churches. The library is partially supported by its large holdings of stocks and bonds. 83

PRICHARD, Louise Gilman. A History of the Chicago Public Library. Master's thesis, University of Illinois, 1928. 128 pp., bibl.
After briefly surveying the predecessors of the Chicago Public Library, the author traces its development, with emphasis on the contributions of its four librarians to 1928: William Frederick Poole, 1873-1887; Frederick H. Hild, 1887-1909; Henry E. Legler, 1909-1917; and Carl B. Roden, 1917-1928. 84

SPENCER, Gwladys S. The Chicago Public Library: Origins and Backgrounds. Doctoral dissertation, University of Chicago, 1939. 470 pp., bibl. Published: University of Chicago, 1943.
Examines the many social forces that influenced the development of the Chicago Public Library in 1872. Dr. Spencer illustrates the public library's dependence on the

whims of local government. She also presents a history
of other libraries in Chicago, describes early leaders in
the Illinois Library Movement, and outlines library legislation in Illinois.   85

Indiana

BEAMON, Mamie. The Origin and Development of the Schools
  Services Department of the Indianapolis Public Library.
  Master's thesis, Indiana University, 1962. 80 pp., bibl.
  The author traces the history of the school library services of the Indianapolis Public Library before 1917, when
  the School Services Department was established, and the
  development of the Department from 1917 to 1962. The
  author finds that the Department's policies were influenced
  and kept in a state of constant evolution by the ever-increasing demands placed on it. The main service of the
  Department is to elementary schools, but community organizations and county schools are served to a lesser extent.   86
FEASTER, Doris Madeline. History of Story Telling in the
  Indianapolis Public Library. Master's thesis, Western Reserve, 1951. 37 pp., bibl.
  The author begins with an essay on the life of Carrie Emma Scott, children's librarian at Indianapolis (1917) and
  editor of an anthology of children's literature. She was
  in considerable demand as a teacher and taught at the
  University of Illinois and the University of Minnesota
  among others. The remainder of the paper is devoted to
  a history of story telling at the Indianapolis Public Library from 1917-1950, and the efforts there to interest
  children in reading.   87
HULL, Thomas V. The Origin and Development of the Indianapolis Public Library, 1873-1899. Master's thesis, University of Kentucky, 1956. 82 pp., bibl.
  The author begins his study with a survey of the cultural
  backgrounds of Indianapolis. He then discusses some early
  predecessors, the first established in 1823, of the Indianapolis Public Library. Finally, he traces the history of
  the public library from its opening in 1873 to the year
  1899. The noted bibliographer Charles Evans, served as
  the Indianapolis librarian from 1872-1878, and again from
  1889-1892. His achievements included an enlightened book
  selection program and completion of the library's first
  printed catalog. An appendix (p. 66-72) includes the Rev.
  Hanford A. Edson's influential sermon "A Plea for a
  Public Library," delivered in November of 1868.   88
LEWIS, Dorothy F. History of the Marion County, Indiana

Library, 1844-1930. Master's thesis, Indiana University, 1954. 54 pp. , bibl.

The Marion County library, established in 1844, served the county's population for more than 86 years before it was replaced by state and city libraries. From the beginning the library developed slowly and the author traces this to the following causes: (1) the small population and the concomitant shortage of funds; (2) difficulties in transportation and communication; (3) defects in the political organization of the library; and (4) the lack of qualified professional librarians. Despite its many difficulties, the Marion County Library lasted longer than any other county library in the state of Indiana.   89

TAYLOR, M. U. Public Library Commission of Indiana, 1899-1925. Master's thesis, University of Kentucky, 1953. 110 pp. Not examined.   90

WALTHER, La Vern Arlene. Legal and Governmental Aspects of Public Library Development in Indiana, 1816-1953. Doctoral dissertation, University of Indiana, 1957. 113 pp. , bibl. (D. A. 58-4833).

Dr. Walther divides her study into four major sections: (1) a survey of the history of the Indiana State Library; (2) the development of library legislation in Indiana; (3) a comparison of public library service in Indiana and in the United States for the years 1945 and 1950; and (4) a consideration of the factors that influenced public library development in Indiana. The author finds that Indiana libraries compare quite favorably with the libraries in the nation as a whole. Like other states, Indiana has found it difficult to provide library service for the rural population. An ever-increasing shift of population from rural to urban areas, and the steady flow of people from the city centers to the suburbs have also posed serious problems for library planners in Indiana.   91

ZIMMERMAN, Mary. A History of the South Bend Public Library from 1888 to 1961. Master's thesis, Catholic University of America, 1962. 65 pp. , bibl.

In this history of the South Bend Public Library, which covers the period from 1888, when the library was established, to 1961, emphasis is placed on the decade 1951 to 1961. Some attention is given to the contributions of outstanding staff members to the library's development, and to the planning of a new building, opened in 1960. 92

Iowa

COUGHLIN, Betty. History of the Davenport Public Library. Master's thesis, Western Reserve, 1952. 57 pp. , bibl.

The first library in Davenport was established in 1839
but soon failed. In 1854 the Young Men's Library Association was founded. In 1901 this library evolved into
the Davenport Public Library and was housed in a new
building built with $75,000 given by Andrew Carnegie.
The collection then numbered slightly over 13,000 volumes;
it now numbers nearly 200,000. The author also includes
a survey of Iowa library history in this study.   93

McGUIRE, Letha Pearl. A Study of the Public Library Move-
    ment in Iowa with Special Reference to Certain Outstand-
    ing and Typical Libraries. Master's thesis, University of
    Illinois, 1929. 147 pp., bibl.
    Describes the development of the public library movement
    in Iowa from 1853, when the first social library was es-
    tablished in the State, to 1929. Overall development of
    public libraries in the State is briefly traced, with em-
    phasis on library legislation, library services, and library
    administration. Detailed treatment is given to four public
    libraries: Des Moines, Sioux City, Davenport, and Web-
    ster City.   94

SNYDER, Esther B. The History and Development of the Mu-
    sic Collection and Department of the Public Library of
    Des Moines. Master's thesis, Western Reserve, 1958.
    82 pp., bibl.
    This study is concerned with the history of the music col-
    lection from 1900 to 1958. The collection was housed in
    an area of the library before it was developed as part of
    the Art and Music Department and finally evolved into a
    major department in its own right. The collection, staff-
    ing and program are all discussed by the author.   95

Kansas

CRUMPACKER, Grace F. Library Legislation and the Library
    Movement in Kansas. Master's thesis, University of Illi-
    nois, 1932. Not examined.   96

Louisiana

MORSE, Dorothea Bignell. The Historical Development and
    Foreclosure of a Public Library. Master's thesis, Univer-
    sity of Mississippi, 1960. 59 pp., bibl.
    This is a history of the Alexandria (Louisiana) Public Li-
    brary, from its establishment in 1907 up to its merger
    with the Rapids Parish Library in 1956. The author ap-
    proached this study with these aims in mind: (1) to eval-
    uate the organization of the public library, with emphasis
    on its history; (2) to evaluate the administration of the

library, with emphasis upon relationships between the library board and the general public; and (3) to consider the failure of the library's services to the public. The author concludes that the library failed due to lack of support, and that the people of Alexandria never made any significant use of the library during its 45-year history. 97

Maryland

BLINKHORN, Margaret Ellen. A History of the Bethesda, Maryland Public Library. Master's thesis, Catholic University, 1963. 50 pp., bibl.
This paper presents a history of the Bethesda Public Library from its origin in 1925 up to 1963. The first library collection consisted of a small collection of books known as the "public library shelf." Later this grew into a community library, and finally it merged with the Montgomery County Library system in 1952. By 1961 the Bethesda Public Library was circulating over 500,000 volumes a year. The author traces the efforts of the Newcomb Club, which established the public library that failed in 1936. In 1938 the tax-supported library was founded. 98

KOCH, June V. The Enoch Pratt Free Library, Its History, Organization, and Service to Readers. Master's thesis, Western Reserve, 1951. 60 pp., bibl.
This study presents a brief history (10 pages) of the Enoch Pratt Library from 1884 to 1950. 99

RICE, Didrikke Moen. A History of the Silver Springs, Maryland Public Library from 1931 to 1951. Master's thesis, Catholic University, 1961. 94 pp., bibl.
Describes the operation for 20 years of the Silver Springs, Maryland Public Library, which was founded in 1931 at the beginning of the Depression. For the first 10 years of its existence the library was supported almost totally by voluntary gifts. Its success is attributed to an industrious and dedicated Board of Trustees, to extensive community support, and to advisory aid received from the Maryland Public Library Commission. Also discussed is the library's role in establishing the Montgomery County Library. 100

Massachusetts

BUCHANAN, Jean Briscoe. Early Directions of the Boston Public Library and the Genesis of an American Public Library Psychology. Master's thesis, Southern Connecticut

State College, 1962. 71 pp., bibl.
This thesis emphasizes the elements that combined to
stimulate the establishment of the Boston Public Library
in 1854, the first public library of any real significance
in the United States. The author analyzes the contrasting
philosophies of the two leading spirits in the library's
early history--George Ticknor and Edward Everett--and
shows how Everett's philosophy not only won out in Boston but also proved highly influential all over America.
The author also devotes some time to the forerunners
of the Boston Public Library--parish libraries, early
academic libraries, social libraries, town and school district libraries. Another chaper, on the Library of the
British Museum, discusses the contrasts between British
and American library philosophy. Finally, the author presents a general survey of library development up to
1938.   101
CLARK, Raymond B., Jr. History of the Talbot County Free
Library, Easton, Massachusetts, 1925-1962. Master's
thesis, Catholic University, 1963. 94 pp., bibl.
This library, established in 1925, was a pioneer in the
state of Massachusetts in the provision of bookmobile service, in establishing close relationships between library
and school, and in children's work. At the beginning it
was housed in one room of an office building. By 1962 it
had much larger quarters but still faced serious space
and staff problems. The author finds that the introduction
of federal and state funds greatly aided the library during
the period 1957-1962.   102
McGOWAN, Owen T. P. A Centennial History of the Fall
River Public Library, 1861-1961. Master's thesis, Catholic
University, 1964. 94 pp., bibl.
This study is divided into three parts: (1) the history of
the Fall River, Massachusetts, Athenaeum (1835-1861),
which evolved into the Fall River Public Library; (2) the
early years of the Public Library (1861-1891); and (3) the
opening of the present library building and the history of
the institution from 1899-1961. The library hit its peak
in the 1920's, when yearly circulation reached 600,000.
After that time services were hampered by serious financial difficulties.   103

Michigan

HELMS, Claxton E. The Historical Foundations and Development of Library Services in Allegan County, Michigan.
Master's thesis, Western Michigan University, 1961. 69
pp., bibl.

The author traces the development of libraries in Allegan
County from their first establishment in the early years
of the 19th century up through 1950, with emphasis on the
19th century. He finds that the successful establishment
of libraries in Allegan County was due in part to the
cultural background of the first settlers. People from New
England and New York made up about two-thirds of the
total population of Michigan in 1837. Most of these settlers
were essentially Puritan in spirit, and had the Puritan
respect for education. Churches, schools and libraries developed rapidly under their influence.   104

HOESCH, Mary Jane. A History of the Grosse Pointe Public
Library. Master's thesis, Western Reserve, 1955. 36 pp.,
bibl.
This study traces library development in Grosse Pointe
from 1928 to 1955, stressing the influence of community
action and interest on the development of library service.
The author presents her account in three main sections:
the early history of the system; the campaigns for a central library and their final success; and the history and
achievements of the main library, which was opened in
1953.   105

Minnesota

GIBSON, Frank Everett. The Effects of the Activities of the
Unions in the Minneapolis Public Library on Library Functions and Administrative Processes, and upon Union Members. Master's thesis, University of Minnesota, 1952. 84
pp., bibl.
This study treats historically the effects of unions upon
library functions and administrative practices, and upon
salaries, working conditions and morale of the union members. The first union influence was felt at the Minneapolis
Public Library in 1935, when the janitors became associated with the AFL. By 1950 even the professional librarians were members of a union. The author finds that
although the union organizations were able to secure very
substantial benefits for their members, union participation
in management was unsatisfactory when it conflicted with
the objectives and spirit of library service.   106

LINCOLN, Sister Mary Edmond. Cultural Significance of the
Minneapolis Public Library in its Origins and Develop-
ment: A Study in the Relations of the Public Library and
American Society. Doctoral dissertation, University of
Minnesota, 1958. 388 pp., bibl. (D.A. 60-974)
This study was undertaken to pinpoint the causal factors
that influenced the development of the Minneapolis Public

Library, and to see whether they were similar to those effecting the development of libraries in the East and Midwest. The author finds that, as in Boston and Chicago, the major factors in Minneapolis were economic ability, an interest in culture, local pride, and popular support for a free library. She traces the history of libraries in Minneapolis from the middle 1800's into the 20th century and is careful to consider that history in relation to the society from which it evolved. The library leaders in Minneapolis seemed to be more pragmatic in approach than their philosophically inclined Eastern counterparts. 107

NYLANDER, Enid Pearce. A History of the Duluth Public Library System. Master's thesis, University of Minnesota, 1962. 171 pp., bibl.
After briefly tracing the history of Duluth from 1853 to 1960, the author describes the evolution of the Duluth Public Library from the reading room established in 1869 to its establishment as a public library in 1890. Seven chapters are devoted to the history of the public library, 1890-1960. A final chapter analyzes the development of the Duluth Public Library branches.   108

Mississippi

DICKEY, Pennie Williams. A History of Public Library Service for Negroes in Jackson, Mississippi, 1950-1957. Master's thesis, Atlanta University, 1960. 50 pp., bibl.
Although the Negro is a tax-paying citizen of the United States, he has often been denied public library services. This denial, tied with a low educational level and a low level of income, has made Negroes less than avid readers. This study, one of many on the history of public library service to Negroes in the South done at Atlanta University, details the efforts that led to the first public library in Jackson, Mississippi, in 1951. The author also describes the library quarters, services and finances relating to library service to Negroes in Jackson.   109

GREEN, Elizabeth Boren. The History and Growth of Lee County Library. Master's thesis, University of Mississippi, 1961. 53 pp., bibl.
This history traces the development of the Lee County Library, Tupelo, Mississippi, from its earliest stirrings to 1960. The first serious attempt at public library development in Tupelo came when Miss Emma Edmonds, an English teacher at Tupelo High School, pushed for the establishment of a small public collection in the high school in 1915. She gained support from a number of club women in the city and the library flourished for two years, until

it was crowded out of the school in 1917. For the next
15 years sporadic enthusiasm for the public library was
evident and in 1934 a W. P. A. project began support of
the library. In 1940 the library began its first bookmobile service, the first professional librarian was hired
in 1947, and in 1948 the library purchased an old bank
building for its first real home. From this point the
author describes the development of branch libraries, and
the evolution of the county library.   110

SPARKS, Eva Charline. People with Books: The Services of
   Northeast Regional Library. Master's thesis, University
   of Mississippi, 1962. 85 pp. , bibl.
   The author devotes the first part of her paper to a brief
   analysis of the influences that led to the development of
   the Northeast Regional Library, in northeastern Mississippi, in 1951. She then traces the development of the
   system from 1951 to 1962. Brief accounts of the development of 13 branches are also included.   111

Nebraska

LENFEST, Grace Evelyn. The Development and Present Status of the Library Movement in Nebraska. Master's thesis,
   University of Illinois, 1931. 147 pp. , bibl.
   In this study the development (to 1931) of the following libraries and agencies is considered: (1) the Nebraska State
   Library; (2) the libraries of the State Historical Society
   and the Nebraska Legislative Reference Bureau; (3) the
   libraries of the University of Nebraska and the four state
   teachers colleges; (4) the public libraries of the State; (5)
   the Nebraska Library Association, and (6) the Nebraska
   Public Library Commission.   112

New Jersey

GALLANT, Estelle F. The History of the Free Library of
   Teaneck, New Jersey. Master's thesis, Pratt Institute,
   1954. 72 pp. , bibl.
   The public library in Teaneck traces its beginnings to the
   small, private collection of Mrs. Archibald N. Jordan.
   Mrs. Jordan, who had made her books available to many
   children and adults, in 1912 asked for and was granted a
   deposit collection of books from the New Jersey State Library. In 1923 Mrs. Jordan and a group of women formed the Teaneck Library Association and opened a library
   in an old renovated slave cabin. In 1927 the property was
   sold at a $15,000 profit, and the money was used to es-
   tablish the Free Public Library of Teaneck, under municipal control. From that time on the library has grown

steadily. The author traces the development of services, collections, staff and physical plant up to 1953.   113

New York

BREEN, Mary H. The Traveling Library Service of the New York Public Library in Richmond and The Bronx; A Descriptive History. Master's thesis, Pratt Institute, 1951. 58 pp., bibl.
The author divides her paper into three major sections. The first deals with the development of the traveling library in the United States from 1907, when pioneer librarian Mary Titcomb drove the first book wagon giving county service, up to the current use of book trucks. The second deals with the Richmond Traveling Library from its inception in 1922 to 1950. The third traces the history of The Bronx Traveling Library from its beginnings in 1928. Both areas used wagons until bookmobiles became available. The author also discusses the physical development of the bookmobile.   114

BULLOCK, Judy Y. A Résumé of the History, Growth, and Development of Library Service to Hospital Patients by the Queens Borough (New York) Public Library. Master's thesis, Atlanta University, 1962. 37 pp., bibl.
In this study library service to hospitals is found to be a relatively recent development. It gained impetus during World War I, when the Department of War induced the A. L. A. to set up libraries in base hospitals to aid in the treatment of disabled veterans. After the war ended, Clarence W. Summer, of the Sioux City Public Library, was the first librarian to establish public library service to hospitals. The Queens Borough Public Library began its first service to the Flushing Hospital in 1933; it lasted until 1947 when the hospital was closed. In 1934 service was extended to several other hospitals, and in 1937 the library initiated service to shut-ins. In 1960 the library was serving many shut-ins plus six hospitals in the area.   115

DAVIS, Joan M. Chemung County Library: Past, Present, and Future. Master's thesis, Pratt Institute, 1954. 76 pp., bibl.
The author devotes the first portion of her paper to the history of the Chemung County Library. In 1923, the Steele Memorial Library Association, located in Elmira, New York, found that it could no longer afford to serve non-city residents. In August of that year the County of Chemung agreed to give financial support to the Steele Memorial Library, in order to provide free library service

throughout the county. The first appropriation was $2,000 and the money was used to establish a special department called the Chemung County Library. The department grew rapidly. In 1949 the Steele Memorial Library was absorbed by the county and renamed the Steele Memorial Library of Chemung County. The Chemung County Library now became the "Extension Department." The author describes the development of services, physical plant, and staff. 116

FANNIN, Gwendolyn Marie. A Résumé of the History, Growth and Development of the Story Hour in the New York Public Library. Master's thesis, Atlanta University, 1958. 47 pp., bibl.
This paper traces the history of the Story Hour at the New York Public Library, from its inception in 1908 up to 1958. Since 1908 the Story Hour has been one of the specialities of the New York Public Library and one of the largest such undertakings in America. 117

GOLDSTEIN, Dorothy. The Library for the Blind of the New York Public Library. Master's thesis, Drexel Institute of Technology, 1953. 49 pp., bibl.
The first part of this paper traces the history of the Library for the Blind, its origin as the privately-funded New York Circulating Library for the Blind (1896-1903), its union with the New York Public Library, and its development from 1903 to 1951. 118

ROLLINS, Ottilie H. The Hepburn Libraries of the St. Lawrence Valley. Master's thesis, Western Reserve, 1960. 113 pp., bibl.
A. Barton Hepburn was a wealthy New York philanthropist and banker, who between 1912 and 1920 established a number of libraries in northern New York State. This thesis covers the history of the seven main Hepburn libraries, located in Colton, Edwards, Lisbon, Madrid, Norfolk and Wandington, as well as four branches administered by the Canton Free Library. The author traces the history of these libraries from 1912 to 1958 and discusses the effects of declining population and decreased revenue on their development. All of the collections remained very small, none of them numbering over 10,000 volumes. 119

WONG, Rita. A History of the Chatham Square Branch of the New York Public Library. Master's thesis, Pratt Institute, 1955. 68 pp., bibl.
The Chatham Square Branch was opened in 1899, and in 1900 it merged with the New York Public Library. In 1903 it moved to the second Carnegie branch building built in New York. The author surveys the development of the library's services and collections from 1899 to 1953. 120

ALDRICH, W. L. B. History of Public Library Service for Negroes in Salisbury, North Carolina, 1937-1963. Master's thesis, Atlanta University, 1964. 72 pp. Not examined.   121

BABYLON, E. R. History of the North Carolina Library Commission. Master's thesis, University of North Carolina, 1954. 176 pp., bibl. Not examined.   122

BATTEN, Sara Storey. The History of the Johnston County Public Library System, 1941-1959. Master's thesis, University of North Carolina, 1960. 88 pp., bibl.
The author first sketches the precursors of the Johnston County Library, North Carolina, 1915-1940, and then devotes the major portion of her research to the growth of the system from 1941 to 1959. The General Assembly passed a bill providing state aid for public libraries in 1941, and under this impetus the citizens of Johnston County moved to unite the county's libraries into a general system. That same year a county librarian was hired and the library began operations with a budget of $3,000. The author describes the difficulties encountered by the new system through the war years, and then traces its consistent development up to 1959.   123

EURY, William. The Citizen's Library Movement in North Carolina. Master's thesis, George Peabody College for Teachers, 1951. 75 pp., bibl.
This paper commences with a brief history of libraries in North Carolina up to 1926. The citizen's library movement had its origin in the North Carolina Library Association, but under the leadership of interested citizens it functioned as a citizen's library movement in the real sense of the word. The state was divided into districts, and these districts formed the working units for bringing the need for more and better libraries to the people. The movement gained impetus slowly, but by 1941, when $100,000 was appropriated for state aid to libraries, it had made considerable advances. By 1950, 95 percent of the state's population had access to the libraries, and long-needed Negro library service had been instituted. 124

GARRISON, Barbara Shepherd. A History of the Concord Public Library of Concord, North Carolina. Master's thesis, University of North Carolina, 1965. 126 pp., bibl.
The author begins this study by presenting a brief history of Concord and Cabarrus Counties in North Carolina. In 1911 several local book clubs, made up of women, banded together to found the Concord Library Association. The women held numerous sales to raise money for the library,

but found that their efforts were barely sufficient to run
the library at even a minimum level. The first "librarian's" salary was $15 a month. By 1922 the struggling li-
brary had only 4,000 books, many of them delapidated.
The library somehow struggled through the depression and
war years, but made little significant headway. In 1960
the book collection was less than half of the size suggest-
ed by the A. L. A. standards; the library also
was badly understaffed, and financed far below the sug-
gested level.   125
HUNTER, Carolyn Paul. A History of the Olivia Raney Library,
    1899-1959. Master's thesis, University of North Carolina,
    1964. 84 pp., bibl.
    The Olivia Raney Library was founded as a public library
    by Richard Beverly Raney in memory of his first wife.
    The North Carolina General Assembly granted it a charter
    in 1899, specifying that it was to serve the white popula-
    tion of the city of Raleigh. In 1927 this charter was amend-
    ed to extend the library's services to the Negro population.
    The library first opened in 1901, and the Raleigh Board of
    Aldermen voted the first appropriation in 1902. The county
    appropriated funds to help the library establish county li-
    brary service in 1926. The author emphasizes the develop-
    ment of the services of the library under three head li-
    brarians: Miss Jennie Coffin, J. S. Atkinson, and Miss
    Clyde Smith.   126
MOORE, Bennie Lee. A History of Public Library Service to
    Negroes in Winston-Salem, North Carolina, 1927-1951.
    Master's thesis, Atlanta University, 1961. 57 pp., bibl.
    The Public Library of Winston-Salem was built with Car-
    negie funds in 1903. It was not until 1927 that the Moses
    Horton Branch was opened on a trial basis to serve Negro
    citizens. In 1931 an old one-room store was rented for
    the Negro branch. By 1951 the Negro branch contained
    10,344 books and circulated 45,415. The author analyzes
    the development of services and collections available to
    Negro readers from 1927 to 1951.   127
MURPHY, Sunshine Burchell. The History of the Rockingham
    County Library, 1930-1955. Master's thesis, University
    of North Carolina, 1956. 123 pp., bibl.
    The author begins with a survey of library development
    in Rockingham County, North Carolina, from 1892, when
    the first circulating library was established, up to 1930.
    She then presents the history of the county library from
    1930 to 1955. The library owed its origin to Mrs. B. F.
    McBane, who in 1930 donated 300 books, a furnished
    cottage to house the books, and funds for a staff. In 1934
    the library became known as the Public Library of

Rockingham County and began to receive county funds.
In 1937 a new headquarters building was constructed and
by 1955 eight branch libraries had been built.   128
STEWART, William LeRoy, Jr. A History of the High Point,
North Carolina, Public Library. Master's thesis, University of North Carolina, 1963. 76 pp., bibl.
This paper traces the history of the High Point Public
Library from its establishment in 1926 up through 1959.
It took fourteen years of sustained effort to get the li-
brary started, and from then on matters became more
difficult rather than simpler. From the very beginning the
library lacked the support of the municipal leaders of High
Point. From 1926 until 1950 they placed numerous ob-
stacles in the path of the library's development. The
author describes the often frustrating efforts of library-
conscious individuals to overcome this resistance.   129
TAYLOR, Joann. Public Library Legislation in the State of
North Carolina, 1897-June 30, 1956. Master's thesis,
University of North Carolina, 1958. 89 pp., bibl.
This study traces the history of the public, public-local,
and private laws relating to public libraries in North
Carolina and analyzes the effects of these laws on library
development in the state. The study covers 57 years--
from 1897, when the first public library was established
by law, to June 30, 1956, when the North Carolina Library
Commission was abolished. An appendix contains a chronological list of legislation relating to North Carolina libraries.   130
WHEDBEE, Mabel Martin. A History of the Development and
Expansion of Bookmobile Service in North Carolina, 1923-
1960. Master's thesis, University of North Carolina, 1962.
60 pp., bibl.
Traces the origins and evolution of bookmobile service in
North Carolina from its start in Durham County in 1923
up to 1960. The author attempts to determine the factors
that stimulated or retarded this development. Special emphasis is placed on the demonstrations by the Library
Commission's book truck, the W. P. A. book trucks, and
on state and federal aid.   131

North Dakota

BRUDVIG, Glenn Lowell. Public Libraries in North Dakota:
The Formative Years, 1880-1920. Master's thesis, University of Minnesota, 1962. 129 pp., bibl.
Libraries came to North Dakota in the 1870's but the public libraries had little success until the turn of the 20th
century. This paper traces in detail the development of

public libraries in the state up to 1920. The author finds
that women's clubs were instrumental in establishing libraries in North Dakota and that they were responsible
for obtaining a library tax levy from the legislature in
1900. Further aid was provided by the Carnegie grants
in the late 19th century. By 1920 public library development had reached a plateau in North Dakota, with libraries in all of the major cities and in many of the small
towns.   132

Ohio (Other Than Cleveland)

ARTHUR, Adah W. A History of the Warder Public Library,
Springfield, Ohio. Master's thesis, Kent State University,
1955. 51 pp., bibl.
This paper traces the history of Springfield and its Warder
Public Library. Brief attention is given to library development from 1841, when the first subscription library was
established, to 1890, when Benjamin Warder paid for the
construction of a free public library building. The major
portion of the paper is devoted to Mr. Warder's library
1890-1954.   133
BATTLES, Frances Mildred. An Account of the Development
of the Public Library Movement in Ohio, with Special
Reference to Some Outstanding Libraries. Master's thesis,
University of Illinois, 1928. Not examined.   134
BAUGHMAN, Ruth Olive. Fifty-three Years of Progress; Public Libraries in Lima, Ohio, 1855-1908. Master's thesis,
Western Reserve, 1954. 92 pp., bibl.
This study traces the evolution of library service in Lima,
Ohio, from the establishment of the first school district
libraries in the middle of the 19th century to the institution of a free public library in 1901, and from there to
1906, when the Carnegie library building was built. It includes a list of book titles in one of the library's early
published catalogs.   135
BOONE, Helen H. A History of the Salem (Ohio) Public Library. Master's thesis, Kent State University, 1962.
73 pp., bibl.
This paper is divided into three major parts: (1) history
of early subscription libraries in Salem from 1814 to
1898; (2) history of the tax-supported Salem Public Library from 1898 to 1961, with emphasis on the growth of
the physical plant and services; and (3) the growth of
financial support for the library and the development of
the book stock.   136
BOWDEN, Clyde Norman. The History of Lane Public Library,
Hamilton, Ohio. Master's thesis, Western Reserve, 1955.

36 pp., bibl.

The Lane Library is one of the oldest public libraries in Ohio. Special state legislation in 1868 permitted the city of Hamilton to accept the gift of a library from one of its citizens, Clark Lane. A brief biography of Mr. Lane and a survey of precursors of the Lane Library are presented in the early chapters. The author then goes on to trace the library's history, 1868-1954. 137

BURTON, Arlynn Schmidt. The Cuyahoga County (Ohio) Library System: A History. Master's thesis, Western Reserve, 1952. 122 pp., bibl.

This study traces the Cayahoga County Library from its conception in 1921 with the passage of the County District Library Bill to its development as one of the largest county libraries in America. The administrations of librarians Amy Winslow (1941-1946) and Raymond C. Lindguist (1946-) are treated in depth. 138

BUZZARD, Ruth Ann. History of Bookmobile Service, Dayton Public Library, Dayton, Ohio. Master's thesis, Western Reserve, 1953. 47 pp., bibl.

This paper treats the history of bookmobile service in Dayton, Ohio, and in Montgomery County, Ohio, from 1923 to the end of 1952. Special emphasis is placed on the ideas and influence of Electra C. Doren, librarian in Dayton 1896-1905 and 1913-1927. A leading library pioneer, she instituted the library's bookwagon--the first one in the state, and one of the earliest in the nation. 139

COLLINS, Lucile T. A History of the East Cleveland Public Library. Master's thesis, Western Reserve, 1951. 41 pp., bibl.

This study covers the period 1904 to 1950, with emphasis on the years 1904-1916. The author offers a brief history of Cleveland and traces the history of the library movement in the United States and Ohio. 140

CRAMER, Jack C. History and Development of Library Services in the Township of Hudson, Summit County, Ohio. Master's thesis, Kent State University, 1950. 80 pp., bibl.

Traces the development of library service in Hudson Township from the first subscription libraries of George Kilbourne and David Hudson (established 1802), through the founding and development of the Hudson Library and Historical Society. In 1910 Mrs. Caroline Babcock presented a $100,000 endowment for the establishment of the Hudson Library and Historical Society, having in mind the initiation of a historical museum and the establishment of a free circulating library to serve the residents of Hudson Township. In addition to a history of the library the author analyzes its relationship with the Western

Reserve Academy Library. 141

DONZE, S. L. History of the Dr. Sloan Library, Zanefield, Ohio. Master's thesis, Western Reserve, 1958. 54 pp., bibl. Not examined. 142

ECKERT, Charlott Jane. A History of the New Philadelphia-Tuscarawas County (Ohio) District Library. Master's thesis, Western Reserve, 1955. 53 pp., bibl.
This paper emphasizes the origins and early development of the library from 1900 to 1937. It traces the development and influence of the Philadelphia Union Club Library Association, a women's organization that lent great support to library development. 143

ELIAS, William D. History of the Reed Memorial Library, Ravenna, Ohio. Master's thesis, Kent State University, 1961. 60 pp., bibl.
After presenting a brief history of Ravenna from 1799 to 1960, the author traces the history of the Ravenna Public Library from 1913 to 1960. Crowded conditions, financial shortages, and a lack of professional help were the library's problems. In 1960 the library contained 30,000 volumes. 144

FLEISCHER, Miriam L. A History of the Rocky River Public Library. Master's thesis, Western Reserve, 1954. 45 pp., bibl.
The author describes the institution of the North Ridge Literary Society in 1877 and traces its evolvement into the Rocky River Public Library in 1925. In 1926 the library was built with a $25,000 gift and a $60,000 bond issue and since that time has developed steadily. In 1952 the Library Board turned down an offer to become the fourth regional branch of the Cuyahoga County Library. 145

FORNEY, Dorothy Jean. The History of the East Palestine Public Library. Master's thesis, Western Reserve, 1954. 42 pp., bibl.
This study covers the span of 34 years from 1920 to 1954. The library was started sometime in 1920 with books from the state traveling library. After several defeats of bond issues, the library was able to erect a new building in 1954 as a result of gifts by the citizens. 146

GOOCH, R. E. History of Birchard Public Library and Sandusky County Extension Service. Master's thesis, Western Reserve, 1957. 67 pp., bibl. Not examined. 147

GOODALE, Grace. History of the Portage County Library, Ohio. Master's thesis, Western Reserve, 1951. 45 pp., bibl.
In 1935 the school board passed a bill creating the Hiram Village School District Public Library. The collection was made up of 150 second-hand books purchased for $35, but

soon was augmented by 2,500 books from the state traveling library. In 1942 a large house was purchased for the
library's new home. The author carries her history through
1950.   148

HARSHFIELD, Lula. The Wagnalls Memorial. Master's thesis,
Western Reserve, 1957. 100 pp., bibl.
This study describes the events surrounding a gift of near-
ly a million dollars by Mabel Wagnalls-Jones in honor of
her father Adam W. Wagnalls (co-founder of the Funk and
Wagnalls publishing company) and her mother Anna Willis
Wagnalls. The $500,000 building, containing some 12,000
volumes, stands in Lithopolis, Ohio, a town of 360 people,
and houses such treasures as a number of original O.
Henry letters.   149

HAZELTINE, Robert Earl. The History of Birchard Library;
Freemont, Ohio, 1874-1950. Master's thesis, Western
Reserve, 1950. 56 pp., bibl.
This study traces the development of the Birchard Library
from 1873, when Sardis Birchard first pondered the idea,
until 1950. Emphasis is laid on the founding and development of the early library. Sardis Birchard donated $50,000
to get the library started. The influence of President
(then Governor of Ohio) Rutherford B. Hayes on the development of the library is discussed.   150

HEIM, Helen R. A History of the Lepper Library of Lisbon,
Ohio. Master's thesis, Kent State University, 1965.
96 pp., bibl.
This paper presents a history of the Lepper Library from
its inception in 1896, due to the efforts of Virginia Lepper, up to 1965. The Lepper Library is one of 26 remaining association libraries in Ohio. In 1965 the book
collection numbered 50,000 volumes.   151

HOPKINS, Laura. The Development of the Local History and
Genealogy Division of the Toledo Public Library. Master's thesis, Western Reserve, 1957. 74 pp., bibl.
In 1939 the Toledo Public became one of the first libraries in the country to establish a separate history and
genealogy division. The first section of the paper is devoted to a brief history of the Toledo Public Library
from its origin in 1838 to 1957. The author then traces
the history of the Division from 1941 to 1956 and indicates
its program aims: (1) to acquire and maintain an excellent history and genealogy collection; (2) to stimulate interest in local history; and (3) to emphasize departmental
participation in historical research.   152

LEWIS, Mary Elizabeth. A History of the Mount Vernon, Ohio,
Public Library, 1888-1949. Master's thesis, Western Reserve, 1950. 56 pp., bibl.

The first three chapters of this paper deal with (1) a sketch of the city of Mount Vernon; (2) early library organizations up to 1888; and (3) the public library from its opening in 1888 to 1900. The remaining three chapters cover the period 1900 to 1949.   153

LOW, Joanne Flora. A History of the Cuyahoga Falls Library Association and the Taylor Memorial Association. Master's thesis, Western Reserve, 1955. 98 pp., bibl.
The Cuyahoga Falls Library Association, founded in 1883 by the poet Edward Rowland Sill, served the community until 1911. It was replaced by the Taylor Memorial Association in 1912. At first a subscription library, Taylor Memorial became a city library during the depression years and is now a county library. The author treats its development up to 1954, when the collection numbered 36,000 volumes.   154

MacCAMPBELL, B. B. History of the Kent, Ohio, Free Library. Master's thesis, Western Reserve, 1950. 98 pp., bibl. Not examined.   155

MESHOT, Genevieve V. A History of the Hubbard Public Library. Master's thesis, Western Reserve, 1949. 23 pp., bibl.
This library, actually a school district library, was first established in 1929, and this paper covers its growth up to 1948. As with many other American small-town libraries, a women's group, the Hubbard Colloquial Forum was very influential in its development.   156

MURRAY, Katherine. History of the Development of Bookmobile Service, Hamilton County, Ohio. Master's thesis, Western Reserve, 1951. 37 pp., bibl.
The author traces the development up to 1950 of the bookmobile service instituted by the Cincinnati Public Library in Hamilton County in 1926. The relation of population trends to the expansion of services is statistically illustrated.   157

MUTSCHLER, Herbert F. The Ohio Public Library and State Aid. Master's thesis, Western Reserve, 1952. 50 pp., bibl.
This study commences with a survey of early Ohio library history (1795-1851) and then considers chronologically the development of state aid in Ohio. The first real step toward solvency for public libraries was the institution in 1934 of a new source of income--the county intangible tax. Robert A. Taft, then a state senator, sponsored the bill. In 1935 $100,000 was granted by the State Assembly to public libraries in Ohio and state aid became a fact. Appropriations were made every year thereafter,

enabling the public libraries to expand their services. 158

NESTLEROAD, Rosemary. A History of Fifty Years of Library Service: Napoleon Public Library, Napoleon, Ohio. Master's thesis, Western Reserve, 1956. 39 pp., bibl.
The author begins this study with a consideration of the subscription library established in Napoleon in 1906. This library was sponsored by the Women's Christian Temperance Union and the membership fee was 25 cents for a three-month period. Readers had some 200 books to select from. One year later another group of women established the Napoleon Library Association, and by 1911 the collection had grown to 1,200 volumes. In 1911 Andrew Carnegie gave the city $10,000 and the Carnegie Free Public Library was built. The author concludes by surveying the administrations of the five librarians who served through 1953: Ora Sheffield, Evelyn Ferris, Leopold Gergely, F. B. Stoughton, and Ada Wells.   159

NOLAN, C. The History of the County Library in Ohio. Master's thesis, Western Reserve, 1949. 31 pp., bibl.
This paper gives a description of Ohio county libraries from 1898 to 1949, with consideration of library legislation and its effects on Ohio library development. The author describes the Brumbach Library in Van Wert County, established in 1898, which is usually considered the first county library in America. Despite the early start, Ohio county libraries developed slowly up to 1940, although trends seem to indicate an accelerated pace since then.   160

REED, Mary Martha. History of the Lakewood Public Library, Lakewood, Ohio: The First Twenty-five Years, 1913-1938. Master's thesis, Western Reserve, 1959. 79 pp., bibl.
The author, after presenting an outline of the history of Lakewood, traces the history of the library in topical form, dealing with such subjects as the book collection, the physical plant, library government, financial support, and personnel. The collection grew to nearly 80,000 volumes by 1938 and the library was operating ten branches in the city schools. The considerable influence of Roena A. Ingham, librarian 1915-1938, is stressed.   161

SATTERFIELD, Helen Cadman. History of Highland County District Library. Master's thesis, Kent State University, 1960. 60 pp., bibl.
Treats chronologically the history of the Highland County District (Public) Library from its beginnings in 1877 to 1959. The author emphasizes the development of the physical plant and the book collection, 50,000 volumes in 1958. She briefly discusses the two branch libraries in Greenfield and Lynchburg.   162

SHEWMAKER, Janet D. History of the Willoughby Public Library, Willoughby, Ohio. Master's thesis, Western Reserve, 1953. 30 pp., bibl.
The study opens with brief sketches of the libraries in Willoughby before 1905, when the public library was established. The author traces the history of the public library to 1952. In 1906 the Circulating Library Society donated its 1,400 books to the new library, and in 1909 a new library building was built with $14,500 given to the city by Andrew Carnegie. In 1947 the library was officially designated the Willoughby Public Library and entered into a contract with the local school board to provide service to the school system. In 1952 the collection numbered 16,000 volumes.   163

SOMERVILLE, Sally A. A Brief History of the Public Libraries of Mentor, Ohio. Master's thesis, Kent State University, 1962. 68 pp., bibl.
A history of libraries in Mentor, Ohio, from 1819 to 1962. Arranged chronologically, this paper treats the following libraries: (1) Mentor Library Company (1819); (2) Mentor Library Association (1875); (3) Mentor Village Library Association (1890); and (4) Garfield Public Library (1927).   164

SPAULDING, Verdabelle Abbott. A History of the Two Public Libraries in Mentor, Ohio. Master's thesis, Western Reserve, 1950. 31 pp., bibl.
The libraries considered here are the Garfield Public Library, the older of the two, which is covered from 1819 to 1927, and the Mentor Township Public Library, from its inception in 1925 to 1935. The history of the predecessors of both libraries is also sketched.   165

SZKUDLAREK, Marie Ellen. Historical Development of Work with Children in the Toledo Public Library. Master's thesis, Western Reserve, 1954. 37 pp., bibl.
The Toledo Library's Children's Department, established in 1899, was one of the pioneers in this area of public library service. The author traces its history, also that of the library itself and the children's library movement in general. In 1918 Miss Ethel C. Wright was named head of the children's department and she was instrumental in its organization and in training children's librarians. By 1952 the Children's Department was circulating 874,000 books annually and had a collection of over 150,000 volumes.   166

TEETER, L. W. A Brief History of the Growth and Development of the Youngstown Library Association, Youngstown, Ohio. Master's thesis, Kent State University, 1956. 53 pp., bibl.

A portion of this paper deals with the history of the Association from 1900 to 1950. The rest of the paper deals with current (1956) operations.   167

THOMAS, Marjorie Evalyn. History of Public Library Service in Jackson County, Ohio. Master's thesis, Kent State University, 1963. 94 pp., bibl.
After a brief history of Jackson County, this paper traces the historical development of the three Jackson County Public Libraries: Jackson Public Library, Welliston Public Library, and Oak Hill Public Library. The three libraries suffered serious financial difficulties from their earliest beginnings and are still quite small.   168

WEIS, Leah Ann. The History of Children's Work at Akron Public Library in Akron, Ohio. Master's thesis, Western Reserve, 1951. 72 pp., bibl.
After presenting a survey of library history in Akron, the author traces the history of the Children's Department from 1900 into the middle of the 20th century. The library was fortunate to have such an industrious, forceful children's librarian as Miss Maude Herndon during the years 1900 to 1920. She was able to garner sufficient monetary support to put the department on a sound footing by the time of her retirement. The department slowed after her departure until 1928, when Miss Harriet W. Leaf was named librarian. She was able to reorganize the department, to make large additions to the collection and to hire numerous children's librarians. Since that time progress has been uniform.   169

WINE, Eugene. The Development of the Dayton Public Library, Dayton, Ohio, 1900-1957. Master's thesis, Western Reserve, 1958. 38 pp., bibl.
The author treats library development in light of the economic and political background of the area. Four major subjects are considered: (1) the library's economic and political background; (2) the story of the main building; (3) branch library development; and (4) changes in services.   170

WOLCOTT, Merlin D. The History and Development of the Sandusky Library Association, Sandusky, Ohio. Master's thesis, Kent State University, 1953. 78 pp., bibl.
Chapter II deals with the social pressures that led to the establishment of libraries in Sandusky as early as 1825. The author traces the evolution of libraries in Sandusky from the Portland Library Association, to the Sandusky Lyceum, to the Philomathesian Society, to the Young Men's Christian Association, and finally to the Sandusky Library Association of 1870.   171

YOUNG, Mary Jo. The Akron Public Library, 1942-1957.

Master's thesis, Western Reserve, 1958. 66 pp., bibl.
This paper describes one of the most active periods of
growth in the Akron Public Library's history. The author
surveys Akron library history from 1834 to 1942 before
beginning a detailed history of the period 1942-1957. Emphasis is placed on the physical features of development.
Little space is given to library personalities; however, the
influence of librarian Russell Munn is readily discernible.   172

YOUNG, Sefville S. History of the Norwalk Public Library
from 1853-1927. Master's thesis, Western Reserve, 1954.
106 pp., bibl.
This paper actually is a history of the antecedents of the
Norwalk Public Library. In 1853 the library came to life
as an integral part of the Whittlessey Academy of Arts
and Sciences. The collection grew slowly and in 1866 it
was merged with the collection of the Young Men's Library and Reading Room Association. In 1867 the collection numbered some 2,000 volumes and began to enjoy
a rather wide patronage. In 1870 the collection of the
Firelands Historical Society was added. In 1903 Andrew
Carnegie granted the city $15,000 for a building, and in
1927 the Association turned the building and its collections over to a new School District Public Library.   173

Ohio - Cleveland

BRADLEY, Nellie V. The Development of Service to Children
in the Cleveland Public Library, with Special Reference
to Perkins Library. Master's thesis, Western Reserve,
1951. 57 pp., bibl.
Chapter I of this study surveys the evolution of children's
library service in America. Chapter II evaluates the influence of William H. Brett, Caroline Burnite, the Library
League, and Effie L. Power on children's work in Cleveland. Chapters III and IV deal with the history of the
Perkins Library, which at its opening in 1908 was the
first in Cleveland devoted exclusively to children. The development of this library is illustrative of the type of ex-
perimentation that took place in the early 20th century. 174

COPELAND, Elizabeth F. A History of Carnegie West Branch
of the Cleveland Public Library. Master's thesis, Western
Reserve, 1954. 51 pp., bibl.
This branch of the Cleveland Public Library was opened
in 1892 in a rented room on the second floor of a building on Pearl Street. The original collection numbered
nearly 5,000 volumes. The author describes the changing
conditions the library faced over a 60-year period. At

first the library served only a wealthy and established class of readers. However, at the turn of the century large groups of transient workers, attracted by burgeoning industry, settled in the area. The author describes the changes made in library service to meet the demands of the new population. 175

GREENE, James Thomas. A History and Description of the Literature Division of the Cleveland Public Library. Master's thesis, Western Reserve, 1954. 110 pp., bibl.
The Literature Division got its start when William Howard Brett initiated a plan for the departmentalization of the Cleveland Public Library. In 1925 the Division moved into modern, convenient quarters in Cleveland's new library. Circulation began to soar in 1928 as spreading unemployment provided more time for reading. With the passing of the depression in 1935, circulation and reference figures decreased. Over the years the staff of the Division has become increasingly involved in community life through sponsorship of poetry readings, book talks to clubs, and membership in civic organizations. 176

INGALLS, Mary Elizabeth. The History and Description of the Philosophy and Religion Division of the Cleveland Public Library. Master's thesis, Western Reserve, 1954. 50 pp., bibl.
Established in 1913, the Philosophy and Religion Division has expanded from its original alcove to a large room on the third floor of the main library, crowded with a collection numbering some 70,000. The first section of this paper is historical in nature, the rest is a description of present (1954) services. 177

MURRAY, Mary Elizabeth. The Branch Library: A Mirror of Its Community, with Case Histories of Several Branches of the Cleveland Public Library. Master's thesis, Western Reserve, 1951. 50 pp., bibl.
This study devotes the first of three sections to the history of branch libraries in Cleveland. After presenting a general introduction, the author traces the history of the following branches: Broadway, Carnegie West, Collinwood, Eastman, Euclid-100th Street, Glenville, Hough, Norwood, Nottingham, Quincy, South Brooklyn, Sterling, Superior, and West Park. 178

NAGY, Mary Catherine. History and Relationship of the Rice Branch Library to Its Hungarian Patrons. Master's thesis, Western Reserve, 1952. 28 pp., bibl.
The author begins by outlining the history of the Hungarian population of Cleveland and then traces the history of the Rice Branch's service to Hungarian patrons since 1916.

From the beginning the demands were great. The author
discovered three major groups using the library: (1) the
aged who never had or would learn English; (2) newcom-
ers who might later master English; and (3) people who
knew English but read Hungarian literature to stay familiar with their original language. The period after 1945
saw a tremendous influx of displaced Hungarians into
Cleveland, and this greatly increased demands for Hungarian materials.   179

PHILLIPS, Virginia. Fifty-six Years of Service to the Foreign-born by the Cleveland Public Library. Master's
thesis, Western Reserve, 1957. 55 pp., bibl.
The author describes the efforts of the Cleveland Public
Library from 1900 to 1956 to aid the foreign-born in their
attempts to become Americanized. Two librarians in the
Cleveland area were prominent in this work: Mrs. May
Sweet, librarian at the Alta Branch (1906-1938) in the
Italian District, and Mrs. Eleanor Ledbetter, librarian
at the Broadway Branch in the Bohemian and Polish area
from 1910-1938. The development of services such as
home visits and special library programs is covered.
After 1940 a shortage of personnel and shifts in the urban
population forced the library to change its approach. 180

SCHRYVER, Norma E. A History of the Business Information
Bureau of the Cleveland Public Library. Master's thesis,
Western Reserve, 1950. 51 pp., bibl.
The Business Information Bureau was initiated in answer
to the demand for a special library service to businessmen. In 1928, Miss Rose Vormelker was brought in to
organize and administer the department. The author outlines her contributions and traces the development of the
department through 1950. The department's success was
immense and became one of the best known services of
the Cleveland Public Library. It was even directly responsible for bringing a number of industries to Cleveland because of the fine business information service
available.   181

SHAMP, B. Kathleen. The Music Section of the Cleveland
Public Library. Master's thesis, Western Reserve, 1954.
53 pp., bibl.
The music section began in 1920 with slightly over a
thousand volumes and a budget of $200-$400. The author
describes the efforts to interest patrons--displays, bibliographies, newspaper publicity, etc. In the late 20's came
the domination of the music field by radio and the author
describes how the library met this awkward situation. A
similar situation arose with phonograph records in the
1940's. In the fifties the library's holdings numbered over

20,000 items. The author concludes with a discussion of
gifts to the library.   182
SHEFFIELD, Helen Gertrude. A Report on the History and
Development of the Library for the Blind of the Cleveland
Public Library. Master's thesis, Western Reserve, 1951.
29 pp., bibl.
The first effort at providing reading material for the blind
in the Cleveland Public Library was made in 1903, when
a small collection of braille books was made available
for loan. Librarian Linda A. Eastman pressed for increased services and by 1913 the collection contained 665
volumes, with a circulation of 421 that year. The appropriations were relatively small until 1932, when the Cleveland Public Library was chosen as a regional center for
the reception of braille books from the government. Under this program the collection grew to 30,647 volumes
in 1950.   183
SILVER, Robert Alan. A Description and History of the Foreign Literature Division of the Cleveland Public Library.
Master's thesis, Western Reserve, 1953. 63 pp., bibl.
In the final portion (20 pp.) of this paper the author
traces the history of the Division from the early 1900's
up to 1950. The Foreign Literature Division gained full
status in 1925. The author describes the influence on the
Division of the wars and the concomitant influx of foreign-
born people.   184
YOCKEY, Robert. The Winged Bequest: An Account of the
Cleveland Public Library's Service to the Incapacitated.
Master's thesis, Western Reserve, 1949. 78 pp., bibl.
This paper describes the efforts of the Cleveland Public
Library to distribute books to the handicapped. The service began in 1936 with aid from the Works Progress
Administration. Shut-ins and invalids were visited and
given books. In 1941 the Frederick W. and Henrietta
Slocum Judd Fund was established, with $519,000 to sup-
port the program, so that "those who cannot run may
read." Services were greatly expanded, and in the last
year covered by this study nearly 4,000 shut-ins were
helped.   185

Oregon

BARRETT, Myrna. History of Oregon Public Libraries. Master's thesis, University of Oregon, 1940. 121 pp., bibl.
The development of public libraries in Oregon is traced
from the establishment of the Library Association of
Portland in 1864 up to 1940. Development was relatively

slow. At the turn of the century, when the women's clubs of the state pushed a law for the tax support of libraries through the legislature, only nine libraries were able to take advantage of it. However, this law stimulated library growth in the state, and by 1913, when the State Library was organized, there were 45 libraries in Oregon. The author discusses financial and personnel developments in the public libraries of Oregon up to 1940, and devotes one chapter to library housing. 186

KIRCHEM, Charleen Ellen. Library Development in Clackamas County, Oregon. Master's thesis, University of Washington, 1952. 60 pp., bibl.
The author devotes the first twenty pages of this study to a survey of library developments in Oregon from the early 1840's up to 1950. The final portion is devoted to short historical accounts of the ten public libraries in Clackamas County. 187

Pennsylvania

AMBLER, B. H. History of the Children's Department of the Free Library of Philadelphia, 1898-1953. Master's thesis, Drexel Institute of Technology, 1956. 60 pp. Not examined. 188

BARKER, Jeanne Welsh. The History and Development of the Monessen Public Library, Monessen, Pennsylvania. Master's thesis, Western Reserve, 1953. 61 pp., bibl.
The study begins with a survey of the town and its environment. Part two traces the history of the Public Library from 1934, when the Monessen Women's Club pushed to establish a library program for the city, up to 1953. The club merged its meager collection with the school district library and thus provided library service to the whole community. 189

DIANA, Joan P. History of the Osterhout Free Library, 1889-1961. Master's thesis, Marywood College, Scranton, Pennsylvania, 1961. 41 pp., bibl.
This paper traces the development of the Osterhout Free Library of Wilkes-Barre, Pennsylvania, from its beginnings in 1889 to 1961. The library was given to the city in 1882 by Isacc Smith Osterhout, a wealthy businessman. When it opened it contained some 10,500 books and was staffed by six people. In 1961 the collection had grown to over 120,000 volumes and the staff numbered 28. The author finds that the Osterhout Library was the beginning of the free public library movement in northeastern Pennsylvania. 190

DIPIETRO, Lawrence N. The Free Library of Philadelphia: Its Formation and Early Physical Growth from 1891 to 1917. Master's thesis, Drexel Institute of Technology, 1952. 46 pp., bibl.

The library conference of 1876, held in Philadelphia, planted the idea of a public library in the minds of the people of that city. However, the city administration seemed satisfied with the numerous semi-public libraries already available to Philadelphia residents. Thus it was not until 1889, when Mr. George Pepper presented $250,000 to the city for a public library, that any action was taken. The library system began official operation in 1891, and in 1894 the 14,356-volume book stock registered a phenomenal circulation of over 60,000. The author discusses the development of the branch system, the services offered by the library, and its efforts to build up the collection. 191

EGOLF, Jean Lois. A History of the Bethlehem Public Library, Bethlehem, Pennsylvania, 1901 to 1954. Master's thesis, Drexel Institute of Technology, 1955. 63 pp., bibl.

The author surveys the history of Bethlehem, Pennsylvania, and discusses the predecessors of the Bethlehem Public Library. In 1900 a group of local women organized the Bethlehem Library Association and started a public subscription library. For the next 20 years subscriptions and gifts were the library's sole means of support, and it encountered numerous financial difficulties. In 1920 the library began to receive public tax funds, and by 1950 was circulating over 120,000 books yearly. The author describes the development of children's work, a branch library system, the physical plant, and the staff. 192

GIRVIN, Catherine M. The Allentown Free Library, A History of Its Growth and Services. Master's thesis, Drexel Institute of Technology, 1954. 58 pp., bibl.

The first part of this paper is devoted to a survey of early library development in Allentown, Pennsylvania. The author reports that as early as 1810 libraries were being established in the city. She treats the history of the Allentown Free Library in three chronological sections: early development, 1912-1929; later development, 1930-1942; and recent growth, 1943-1953. Within each section emphasis is placed on the development of the physical plant, financial support, book collection, staff and library services. 193

KEIM, Aldine. The History of Cambria Free Library, Johnstown, Pennsylvania, 1925-1951. Master's thesis, Drexel Institute of Technology, 1952. 46 pp., bibl.

This paper presents a brief summary of the early history

of the Cambria Free Library (1870-1925), a description
of the community it served, and a history of the institution from 1925 to 1951. Emphasized are administrative
organization, financing, and special services such as
children's services, bookmobile services, and special
collections.   194

KLUGIEWICZ, E. Short History of the Erie (Penn.) Public
Library. Master's thesis, Western Reserve, 1953. 33
pp., bibl. Not examined.   195

MEYER, William P. A History of the Reading, Pennsylvania,
Public Library, and Its Services to the Community, 1898-
1952. Master's thesis, Drexel Institute of Technology,
1953. 55 pp., bibl.
The author traces library history in Reading from 1808,
when a subscription library was founded, up to 1952. The
subscription library later evolved into the Reading Library (1868), and in 1898 was opened to the public and
renamed the Reading Public Library. Each of five chronological chapters emphasizes the development of staff, facilities, collections and services.   196

RYBERG, H. Theodore. Warren Public Library; A History.
Master's thesis, Western Reserve, 1957. 53 pp., bibl.
Discusses the development of the Warren Public Library,
which originated in a library association founded in 1831.
The library suffered serious financial difficulties, but
many benefactors helped ease the burden. In 1902 a Children's Room was opened, and in 1956 the collection numbered 80,000 volumes.   197

SMITH, Mabel H. Three Rural Libraries of Chester County,
Pennsylvania; A Historical Survey of Their Development
and Services to the Community. Master's thesis, Drexel
Institute of Technology, 1950. 42 pp., bibl.   198
This study traces the history of three rural libraries
within fifteen miles of each other in Chester County,
Pennsylvania. The libraries treated are the Oxford Public
Library, the West Grove Library, and the Bayard Taylor
Library of Kennett Square. All three libraries were es-
tablished around 1900, and they have remained quite
small.   198

TUCK, Rhoda Shearer. Evolution of the Chester County Library; A History. Master's thesis, Drexel Institute of
Technology, 1954. 65 pp., bibl.
This paper is divided into three major portions: (1) a
history of Chester County, Pennsylvania; (2) a history of
the immediate predecessor of the Chester County Library--
the Public School Circulating Library (1897-1930); and (3)
the history of the Chester County Library, 1928-1954.
The author finds that the County Library was a young

institution in an old and conservative community and that
progress and change were effected very slowly.   199

WHITNEY, Ellen Mae. History of the Norristown (Penn.) Public Library. Master's thesis, Drexel Institute of Technology, 1955. 51 pp., bibl.
This paper traces the history of the Norristown Public
Library from its beginnings as a subscription library in
1794 to its status as a public library in 1955. After a
brief historical sketch of Norristown, the author treats
the library in three chronological periods, with emphasis
on the following points: housing, collections, circulation,
financial support, and staff.   200

WINGER, Anna Kathryn. History of the Huntingdon County Library, Huntingdon, Pennsylvania, 1935-1953. Master's
thesis, Drexel Institute of Technology, 1954. 52 pp., bibl.
This paper includes a brief analysis of the Huntingdon
County Library, a description of the county it serves,
and a history of the library for its 18 years of existence,
1935 to 1953. The library in 1953 was unable to gain
much support from the public and thus failed to win a
referendum calling for increased library appropriations.   201

Rhode Island

HARDING, Sister Mary Faith. A History of the Providence
Public Library, Providence, Rhode Island, from 1878 to
1960. Master's thesis, Catholic University, 1964. 75 pp.,
bibl.
The author begins by sketching the early history of libraries in Providence from 1838 to 1879. In 1838, Francis Wayland, who promoted one of the earliest tax-supported libraries in America, spoke before the members
of the Providence Athenaeum and urged them to extend
their facilities to all the citizens of Providence. Despite
his efforts the city had to wait until 1878 before a public
library was established. It began service with some
10,000 volumes and a full-time librarian. The author discusses in detail the development of the collections, the
construction of a new building in 1896-1900, and the services offered by the library.   202

South Carolina

JARRELL, Penelope Hampton. The Development of the County Library System in South Carolina from 1929 to 1943.
Master's thesis, University of North Carolina, 1955. 70
pp., bibl.

This paper traces the history of county library development in South Carolina from 1929, when the State Public Library Association was established by law, to 1943, when the first appropriations were made. The author finds that in the early stages of development, the people were indifferent toward the service until the WPA gave extensive support to the program in 1930. The author is concerned mainly with broad trends and mentions individual libraries only when they influenced state-wide patterns.   203

South Dakota

CROUCH, Mary Lois. The Library Movement in South Dakota with Special Reference to Some Outstanding Libraries. Master's thesis, University of Illinois, 1930. 152 pp., bibl.
Traces the development of the library movement in South Dakota from Territorial Days to 1930, with attention to advancement through library legislation. A general survey of library development in South Dakota is presented, with a more detailed account of several representative libraries. Emphasis is placed on library service and administrative methods. The libraries receiving detailed treatment are the university libraries at the University of South Dakota and at South Dakota State, and the public libraries in Aberdeen, Ipswich, Lead, Rapid City, Sioux Falls, and Tyndall.   204

Tennessee

BUCK, James Peek. A History of the Library Resources of Putnam County. Master's thesis, Tennessee Polytechnic Institute, 1961. 87 pp., bibl.
This paper is concerned with the history of library resources in Putnam County, Tennessee, and the present status of those resources. The historical half of the paper is divided into two major sections. The first is a study of the early school resources of Putnam County that might have influenced the development of libraries. Andrew College, Washington Academy, and Dixie College are among the schools discussed. The second section deals with the early public library resources that have influenced the present (1961) system. The author finds that the early schools had no libraries to speak of and that students had to depend on faculty libraries. Lack of financial support, which led to the demise of many private schools, also hampered library development. The

church and school organizations were most influential in
providing public libraries. The Episcopal Church established the first in 1914.   206
GOVAN, James Fauntleroy. The History of the Chattanooga
  Public Library, 1905-1950. Master's thesis, Emory University, 1955. 141 pp., bibl.
  The author traces the antecedents of the Chattanooga Public Library and describes socio-economic conditions in
  the city. In 1902 Andrew Carnegie pledged $50,000 for a
  public library in Chattanooga, and in 1905 the library
  opened with a collection of 3,700 volumes. In 1906 a
  children's room was opened, and in 25 years it circulated
  nearly 700,000 volumes. In 1910 Carnegie's offer of
  $15,000 for a Negro library if the local government
  would meet certain requirements was turned down. It was
  not until 1913 that a Negro branch was established, and
  service to colored people was to prove a stubborn problem. The author describes the library's unique cooperative arrangements with the University of Chattanooga,
  the efforts of Julius Rosenwald on behalf of the library
  during the depression, and the development of a school
  library branch as part of the library system.   206
HANSBROUGH, Irene Cross. Public Library Service to Ne-
  goes in Knoxville, Tennessee. Master's thesis, Atlanta
  University, 1959. 66 pp., bibl.
  The author begins by briefly sketching the history of library service to Negroes in the United States. She then
  outlines the history of the Knoxville Public Library System from 1885 to 1957, and traces the history of public
  library service to Negroes in Knoxville 1917-1957. Library service to Negroes was centered in the two Negro
  branch libraries (Murphy and Carnegie) until 1950, when
  Knoxville's libraries were integrated.   207
HOFFMAN, Rheba Palmer. A History of Public Library Services to Negroes in Memphis, Tennessee. Master's thesis, Atlanta University, 1955. 54 pp., bibl.
  This study traces the history of library service to Negroes in Memphis from its beginnings in the early 1900's
  up to 1955. The author finds that services to Negro readers have been haphazard and insignificant, and that Memphis has lagged far behind other southern cities in the
  provision of library service to its Negro residents. 208
McCRARY, Mary Ellen. A History of Public Library Service
  to Negroes in Nashville, Tennessee, 1916-1958. Master's
  thesis, Atlanta University, 1959. 42 pp., bibl.
  The first library in Nashville was established in 1844 as
  a mercantile library; it became a free public library in
  1901 through a donation from Andrew Carnegie. Negroes

were not allowed the use of this library, and it was not until 1916 that a Negro branch was finally opened in Nashville. This library proved unsatisfactory for a number of reasons and it was sold in 1949. In 1950 the Nashville Public Library and all of its branches were opened to Negroes as well as white patrons. 209

Texas

ALLEN, Dorothy Louise. The Kemp Public Library: A History, 1896-1963. Master's thesis, University of Texas, 1965. 138 pp., bibl.
Traces the origin and development of the Kemp Public Library, Wichita Falls, Texas. The early attempts to found a library in the latter part of the 19th century culminated in the early part of the 20th century with the building of the present library. The growth of this library to 1963, with emphasis on collections and services, is discussed. 210

BARNES, G. S. History of Public Library Service to Negroes in Galveston, Texas, 1904-1955. Master's thesis, Atlanta University, 1957. 42 pp. Not examined. 211

CODY, Ninna B. Historical Development of Public Libraries in Gregg County, Texas. Master's thesis, East Texas State College, 1959. 83 pp., bibl.
This study traces the history of the public libraries in Gregg County from the beginnings in the early 30's until 1959. The Woman's Chamber of Commerce worked for establishment of the county's first public library in 1930. The collection opened with around 1,000 volumes and circulated over 7,000 the first year. Later Mr. and Mrs. W. R. Nicholson gave the city a building and $1,000 for a Nicholson Memorial Library. In 1933 the people of Longview voted to support the library with city funds. The three main libraries of the county--Nicholson Memorial Library (1932), The Kilgore Public Library (1939), and the Gladewater Public Library (1937)--were merged into the Gregg County Library system in 1944. There have been few financial difficulties since the oil-rich area has an exceedingly high tax base. 212

GILLESPIE, Richard Charles. La Retama Public Library: Its Origin and Development, 1909-1952. Master's thesis, University of Texas, 1953. 96 pp., bibl.
This study traces the development of the La Retama Public Library in Corpus Christi, Texas, from 1909 to 1952. Chapter I analyzes the historical, cultural, and economic conditions out of which the library grew. Chapter II covers the library's embryo stage and its many difficulties.

The third chapter deals with the library's becoming in 1927 a unit of the city government. Chapter IV deals with the library's building program, which aroused considerable public controversy. Chapter V summarizes the paper. Mr. Gillespie concludes that after 43 years of existence the library had not reached a very successful position, and then presents the reasons for the library's slow and erratic development. 213

MASON, Lena Grimmett. The Founding of the Beaumont, Texas, Public Library, 1870-1926. Master's thesis,Texas State College, 1951. 65 pp., bibl.

The author sets out to trace the events that led to the establishment of the Tyrrell Public Library, Beaumont, Texas, in 1926. The first chapter is devoted to a socio-economic survey of the community 1870-1926, and the next several chapters deal with the events immediately preceeding the establishment of the library in 1926. The author was particularly interested in finding out if individual philanthropy, or a strong desire on the part of many people, was the main influence on library development in Beaumont. She found that both factors were present. 214

SMITH, Mary Helen Kennedy. A History of the Libraries of Bonham, Texas. Master's thesis, East Texas State College, 1963. 109 pp., bibl.

Bonham, Texas, had a population of only 7,357 people in 1960, and yet had five distinct types of library services available to its citizens. The author traces the history of the following libraries: (1) the Bonham public school libraries; (2) the Bonham Public Library (1901-1963); (3) The Library of the Veteran's Administration Center; (4) The Sam Rayburn Library (1957-1963); and (5) four church libraries in Bonham. 215

SUHLER, Samuel Aaron. The Austin Public Library, 1926-1956. Master's thesis, University of Texas, 1959. 72 pp., bibl.

The author briefly traces a 25-year effort to establish a public library in Austin, Texas, an effort frustrated by legislative opposition, a lack of city funds, and a lack of widespread popular support. A small subscription library finally was opened in 1926; in 1928 it became the Austin Public Library. For the next five years library development was rapid, but tended to slow down after 1933. The author analyzes this gradual growth period (1933-1956), and discusses the development of staff, book collections, physical plant and services. 216

Virginia

BRANDT, Beverly S. The Alexandria, Virginia, Library: Its History, Present Facilities, and Future Program. Master's thesis, Catholic University, 1950. 94 pp., bibl.
The author has divided her subject into three major periods. The first covers the history of the library from its hesitant beginnings as a subscription library in 1794 to the dispersal of the library's collection during the Civil War. The second period covers the attempts to revive the library after the way and the establishment of the public library in the 1930's. The final section treats the public library's development up to 1950. Since 1937 the library has shown a steady growth to nearly 27,000 volumes. 217

ELLIOTT, Mary E. The Development of Library Service in Fairfax County, Virginia, since 1939. Master's thesis, Drexel Institute of Technology, 1951. 57 pp., bibl.
This study traces the development of the Fairfax County Public Library System from 1939 to 1951. The Fairfax County Public Library System, as it was established in 1939, offered the first organized library program in the county. It was found that the progress of the library was rapid and extensive. For instance, circulation grew from 24,000 in 1940-1941 to 170,000 in 1949-1950. The author pinpoints problems and successes in the library's history and concludes with suggestions for improving the system. 218

MOYERS, Joyce Catherine. History of the Rockingham Public Library, Harrisonburg, Virginia. Master's thesis, North Carolina, 1959. 116 pp., bibl.
The Rockingham Public Library is a regional library serving the city of Harrisonburg and the counties of Rockingham and Page in Virginia. The Harrisonburg Kiwanis Club was instrumental in promoting the organization of the Rockingham Library Association in 1928, and in 1952 a new library building was constructed entirely from funds derived from public subscriptions. Originally the library was supported by donations, but later received public funds. The author traces the development of the library from 1928 to 1955, with special emphasis on the planning of the new building and the efforts to expand services through state aid. 219

Washington

HAKE, Shirley Dean. A History of Library Development in Kittitas County, Washington. Master's thesis, University of Washington, 1953. 55 pp., bibl.
Kittitas County was settled in 1867 and the author briefly

traces its development from that time until 1953. The
author then traces library development in the county from
1890, when W. W. Bonney opened a newspaper reading
room in Ellensburg, until 1950. Three libraries are covered in some detail: the Carnegie Library of Ellensburg,
begun in 1908; the Cleelum Public Library, begun in 1914;
and the Roslyn Public Library, which got its start in
1898. All three libraries developed slowly and suffered
from serious financial shortages.   220

NEWSON, Harry Edwin. Fort Vancouver Regional Library; A
Study of the Development of Public Library Service in
Clark and Skamania Counties, Washington. Master's thesis,
University of Washington, 1954. 144 pp., bibl.
A brief overview of Clark and Skamania Counties is presented and the author traces the history of early library
development in the two counties. Emphasis is on the development of the Fort Vancouver Regional Library, 1940-
1954. This study describes the operations of the headquarters library and the steps that led to the unification
and development of services in the two counties; little is
said of branches and bookmobile services.   221

ORR, Maryde Fahey. Development of the Walla Walla Public
Library. Master's thesis, University of Washington, 1953.
62 pp., bibl.
This paper traces the development of library interest in
Walla Walla, Washington, from 1865, when the Walla Walla Library Association was founded, to 1950. The first
library, established in 1867, fell into neglect in 1890. It
was not until 1896, when the Women's Reading Club of
Walla Walla raised $1,000 to establish a library, that
the city again had library service. In 1904 the Walla Walla Public Library was established and Andrew Carnegie
gave $25,000 to the city for the construction of a build-
ing. In 1940 the collection had grown to nearly 30,000
volumes. The author goes on to describe the financial
and space problems the library encountered from 1945
to 1950.   222

PITCHER, Patricia Mae. A Historical Study of Library Development in Chelan County, Washington. Master's thesis,
University of Washington, 1952. 67 pp., bibl.
The author sets out to show the relation between economic
development in Chelan County and the development of libraries. One-third of this paper is devoted to the economic development of the county. The remainder contains
individual treatments of five town libraries and the 20
branches of the Chelan County Library, which was established in 1944.   223

STROTHER, Jane Voss. The Development and the Adequacy of

the Library as an Institution in the State of Washington.
Master's thesis, University of Washington, 1938. 156 pp.,
bibl.
The first 25 pages of this paper are devoted to a survey
of the development of the State Library of Washington and
the other public libraries of the state. The State Library
was established in 1853, while the first public libraries
appeared in the 1890's.   224

WARD, Barbara Anne. A History of Public Library Development in Whitman County, Washington. Master's thesis,
University of Washington, 1960. 155 pp., bibl.
Traces the development of public libraries in Whitman
County, Washington, from the establishment of the first
libraries in the 1860's up to 1960. The study is broken
down into four major segments: (1) the cultural, economic
and social influences that effected the development of public libraries, 1868-1880; (2) the growth of independent libraries of all kinds in the county from 1880 to 1905; (3)
the introduction of the public library, its early organization and development, 1906-1940; and (4) the trend toward
larger units of service and the rise of extension work,
1940-1960.   225

West Virginia

WADE, B. A. History of the Waitman Barbe Public Library
of Morgantown, West Virginia, 1926-1956. Master's thesis,
Western Reserve, 1957. 46 pp., bibl. Not examined. 226

Wisconsin

SAUCERMAN, Kathryn. A Study of the Wisconsin Library
Movement, 1850-1900. Master's thesis, University of Wisconsin, 1944. Not examined.   227

College and University Libraries

General Studies

BOLL, John Jorg. Library Architecture 1800-1875; A Comparison of Theory and Buildings with Emphasis on New
England College Libraries. Doctoral dissertation, University of Illinois, 1961. 447 pp., bibl.
Dr. Boll devotes the first part of this study to background
material, the second to influential contemporary foreign
literature, and the third to the buildings themselves, plus
important American library planners. The final section is
a topical survey of the work in general. The author chose

90

seven colleges for his study: Amherst, Brown, Harvard, Yale, Mount Holyoke, Wesleyan, and Williams. Dr. Boll found that writers and planners were very concerned with the protection of the library's collection, and that this influenced them greatly during the period 1800-1875. 228

BROUGH, Kenneth J. Evolving Conceptions of Library Service in Four American Universities: Chicago, Columbia, Harvard, and Yale, 1876-1946. Doctoral dissertation, Stanford University, 1949. 370 pp. , bibl. Published: University of Illinois Press, 1953.
After briefly sketching the history of American college library development to 1876, Dr. Brough analyzes the evolution of concepts of library administration in four American universities from 1876 to 1946. The significance of the four libraries, their book collections, their librarians, their clientele, and the services offered are all topics discussed. 229

CHURCH, Frances Elizabeth. A Historical Survey of the Libraries in a Group of State Normal Schools Prior to 1900. Master's thesis, Columbia, 1931. 118 pp. , bibl.
This study presents a picture of library development in a varied group of state normal schools. The East is represented by two states, Massachusetts and New York, where some of the earliest normal schools were established. Alabama and Texas were chosen to represent the South. Indiana, Michigan, Kansas, Colorado and Nebraska represent the Middle West, where the greatest development has come about. California and Washington represent the Pacific Slope. The author describes 14 libraries in terms of the book collection and its administration; the librarian, and the library room. 230

ERICKSON, Ernest Walfred. College and University Library Surveys, 1938-1952. Doctoral dissertation, University of Illinois, 1958. 459 pp. , bibl. (D. A. 58-5412)
This study attempts to trace the effectiveness of library surveys by experts in bringing about beneficial results to the surveyed library. Twelve surveys were studied, beginning with the first major survey in America at the University of Georgia in 1938. The author found that the surveys were successful in a majority of instances in influencing change, and in prompting an increased library consciousness on the part of librarians, faculty, and administration. 231

GELFAND, Morris Arthur. A Historical Study of the Evaluation of Libraries in Higher Institutions by the Middle States Association of Colleges and Secondary Schools. Doctoral dissertation, New York University, 1960. 449 pp., bibl. (D. A. 61-324)

This study concerns itself with a historical analysis of the evolution and influence of the policies and procedures aimed at the evaluation of libraries in colleges and universities seeking accreditation from the Middle States Association. Dr. Gelfand follows the twists and turns of the path the Association took up to 1960, and then presents conclusions and recommendations based on his findings, part of which were derived from a questionnaire sent to the librarians of all institutional members of the Association. 232

HARDING, Thomas S. College Literary Societies: Their Contribution to Higher Education in the United States, 1815-1876. Doctoral dissertation, Chicago, 1957. 382 pp., bibl. One chapter of this paper analyzes the influence of college literary societies on academic library development from 1815-1876.

KNOER, Sister Mary Margaret Agnes. A Historical Survey of the Libraries of Certain Catholic Institutions of Learning in the United States. Master's thesis, University of Illinois, 1930. 114 pp., bibl.
Studies briefly the development of libraries in 16 Catholic colleges and universities to 1930. The author found that collections were usually small, dated, and used mainly by the faculty. Major improvements were made after the organization of the Library Section of the Catholic Educational Association in 1923. 234

KULP, Arthur Claude. The Historical Development of Storage Libraries in America. Master's thesis, University of Illinois, 1953. 40 pp., bibl. Published: ACRL Microcard #12.
After a brief survey of book storage problems from ancient to modern times, the author describes present-day compact book storage techniques. Six working systems are described in some detail: (1) Iowa State College Library; (2) Cornell University Library Storage Collections; (3) University of Kentucky; (4) New England Deposit Library; (5) Mid-West Inter-library Center; and (6) The Hampshire Inter-library Center. 235

ORR, Robert S. Financing and Philanthropy in the Building of Academic Libraries Constructed Between 1919 and 1958. Master's thesis, Western Reserve, 1959. 87 pp., bibl.
The author details the means of financing 61 college and university library buildings built during 1919-1958. The author found that large benefactions characterized the period prior to 1930, while during the 1930's many state colleges and universities gained libraries through the use of Works Progress Administration funds. After 1940

WPA was curtailed and little building was done until after the war. From then to 1958 most state institutions built libraries with state funds, while private institutions usually depended on a large gift from one individual.   236

POWELL, Benjamin Edward. The Development of Libraries in Southern State Universities to 1920. Doctoral dissertation, University of Chicago, 1946. 233 pp., bibl.
Surveys the history of libraries in the state universities of Alabama, Georgia, Louisiana, Mississippi, North Carolina, South Carolina, Tennessee and Virginia from 1795 to 1920. The author finds that although libraries were considered vital by most of the universities, they were beset by financial difficulties up through the 19th century. The Civil War, Reconstruction, low per capita incomes, segregation and the establishment of specialized institutions also contributed to the retardation of library development in southern state universities through 1900. A final chapter compares data from the eight libraries studied with state university libraries in California, Illinois, Michigan, Minnesota, and Wisconsin.   237

REYNOLDS, Helen Margaret. University Library Buildings in the United States, 1890-1939. Master's thesis, University of Illinois, 1946. 88 pp., bibl.
Presents a historical interpretation of the development of university library buildings in the United States from 1890 to 1939. Twenty-seven universities and their 38 library buildings are discussed. The author outlines the extensive development library buildings underwent, from very simple structures in which the library usually occupied one floor, to complex buildings of several stories with up to 28 stack levels. The author includes numerous plates, illustrating the buildings being described.   238

SMITH, Jessie Carney. Patterns of Growth in Library Resources in Certain Land-Grant Universities. Doctoral dissertation, University of Illinois, 1964. 227 pp., bibl. (D.A. 65-917)
This study sets about to determine what influence such factors as (1) curriculum development; (2) financial support; (3) size of collections; and (4) the development of departmental libraries in science and technology, had on the growth of library collections in a selected group of land-grant institutions. Comparisons were made between the libraries of Purdue and Indiana, Michigan State and the University of Michigan, Iowa State and the University of Iowa. Dr. Smith also compared the libraries of the University of Illinois with those of Ohio State University to ascertain growth patterns in land-grant institutions,

which are also the largest state supported schools in their states. The data gathered covers from 1870 to 1960, with emphasis on the period 1930-1960. The author found that the land-grant institutions were consistently behind comparable state universities in collection building.   239

STORIE, Catherine Penniman. What Contributions Did the American College Society Library Make to the History of the American College Library? Master's thesis, Columbia University, 1938. 116 pp., bibl.
The author of this study had a fourfold purpose in mind: (1) general study of the value of college society libraries; (2) specific analysis of the collections of the Peithologian and Philolexian Societies at Columbia University; (3) a preliminary investigation to determine which colleges had societies, and hence probably society libraries; and (4) which of these society libraries had catalogs, especially printed catalogs, and where they were located. The study covers the period from 1790 to 1900. The author finds that the society library grew up to fill needs resulting from a rigid and limited curriculum, and that it appeared to be a substitute for, rather than a supplement to, the main library. It was found that 80 percent of all the colleges flourishing in 1830 had society libraries, and nearly half of these had collections larger than their college libraries. By 1851 only about 55 percent of the colleges reported society libraries. Appendix A is a list of colleges that had society libraries.   240

STRAUSS, Lovell Harry. The Liberal Arts College Library, 1929-1940: A Comparative Interpretation of Financial Statistics of Sixty-Eight Representative and Twenty Selected Liberal Arts College Libraries. Master's thesis, University of Chicago, 1942. 125 pp., bibl.
This study interprets the financial statistics of 88 liberal arts college libraries from 1929 to 1940. It traces changes in college library support through an analysis of standard recorded statistics. Such factors as enrollments, library expenditures, size of library staff, book budgets, size of collections, growth per year, are considered. Data was gathered from questionnaires and published reports.   241

THURBER, Evangeline. The Library of the Land-Grant College, 1862-1900: A Preliminary Study. Master's thesis, Columbia University, 1928. 84 pp., bibl.
This paper traces the rise and development of the libraries in American land-grant colleges from the passage of the Morrill Act in 1862 to 1900. The author surveys the development of the agricultural colleges and experiment stations and traces the development of their libraries.

In the beginning faculty members acted as part-time librarians, the collections were small and the services were meager. The passage of the Morrill Act provided the financial backing necessary to hire full-time librarians and to increase book collections and services. The Hatch Act in 1887 provided an equal impetus for the experiment stations. The author finds that when experiment station collections were consolidated with the main library the development was smoother and more extensive. Numerous tables illustrating the growth of the collections, the budgets, and facilities of American land-grant college libraries are included.

Local Studies Arranged by State.

Arizona

HEISSER, Wilma A. A Historical Survey of the Phoenix College Library; Phoenix, Arizona, 1925-1957. Master's thesis, Arizona State College, 1958. 80 pp., bibl.
This study presents a history of the Phoenix College Library from its inception in 1925 to the close of 1957. For five years after its establishment in 1920, the college had no library; students had to use the high school library. In 1925, 250 books were transferred from the Phoenix High School Library, and the college library got its start. By 1930 the book stock was up to 4,000 volumes and in 1937 a $3,000 grant from the Carnegie Foundation greatly added to the library's holdings. In 1939 the library was moved into a separate building for the first time. The author discusses the problems faced by the college library, mainly financial, and concludes with a survey of current services (1957).   243

California

SMITH, Dora. History of the University of California Library to 1900. Master's thesis, University of California, 1930. 168 pp., bibl., index. Published: ACRL Microcard #21.
After briefly sketching the history of the University of California, the author traces the history of the library from its beginnings in 1862, as part of the College of California, up to 1900. The author treats her subject under three major heads: the general administration of the library, the collections, and the staff.

Connecticut

BROOKS, Robert Edward. The Yale University Law School Library: Its History, Organization and Development, 1824 to 1962. Master's thesis, Southern Connecticut State College, 1965. 114 pp., bibl.
The Yale Law Library was officially opened in 1824 with a collection of 2,000 volumes. It has grown to be one of the finest legal collections in the world, with holdings of over 450,000 volumes. The author discusses the following: (1) a brief history of the Yale Law School and its organization, (2) the origin and history of the Law School Library, (3) departmental organization of the Law Library, (4) the library's book collection, (5) the classification scheme, and (6) the services offered by the Law Library. 245

COLLA, Sister Maria Beatrice. A History of the Pope Pius XII Library, St. Joseph College, West Hartford, Connecticut, 1932-1962. Master's thesis, Catholic University of America, 1964. 108 pp., bibl.
This study is a historical and statistical study of the library of a small women's college. Chapters dealing with the following topics are included: (1) housing, (2) administration and finances, (3) book and periodical collection, (4) technical services, and (5) public services. 246

District of Columbia

BEACH, Sister Francis Mary. A History of the Library of Trinity College, Washington, D. C. Master's thesis, Catholic University, 1951. 76 pp., bibl. Published: ACRL Microcard #41.
Presents a historical and statistical picture of the development of the library of a Catholic liberal arts college for women from 1900 to 1950. The author analyzes the growth of its book collection in comparison to the growth and curriculum development of Trinity College. She also discusses how the library faced administrative, housing, and financial problems. 247

CHAMBERLAIN, Lawrence Carlton. Georgetown University Library; 1789-1937. Master's thesis, Catholic University of America, 1962. 104 pp., bibl.
The author divides his paper into three major sections. The first deals with the library from its beginnings in 1789 up to the Civil War. The second covers the period from the close of the Civil War to 1889, and the third traces the library's history from 1889 to 1937. In the beginning the library's growth was stimulated by gifts and donations, especially those of the founder of the Georgetown college, John Carroll. By 1831, the 12,000 volumes in the collection ranked Georgetown University's library

in the top ten in America. The author also analyzes the
contributions of librarians Henry Shandelle (1895-1922) and
Arthur O'Leary (1924-1935).   248

DUNCAN, Anne McKay. History of Howard University Library,
1867-1929. Master's thesis, Catholic University, 1951. 97
pp., bibl. Published: ACRL Microcard #42.
Traces the history of the Howard University Library from
its inception in 1867 to 1929. The library began with a
few books located in one room, but by 1929 contained
nearly 50,000 volumes. A new building was provided by
a Carnegie Grant in 1910. The author analyzes the influence of librarian Edward C. Williams on the library's
development and indicates the effects of Congressional
support after 1879.   249

Georgia

LeBOONE, Elizabeth. A History of the University of Georgia
Library. Master's thesis, University of Georgia, 1955.
122 pp., bibl.
The six chapters of this paper treat these topics: (1) early
history of the library; (2) middle period and Civil War
times; (3) literary society libraries; (4) growth and development, 1866-1904; (5) development 1904-1938; and (6)
reorganization and growth, 1938-1952.   250

SATTERFIELD, Virginia. The History of College Libraries
in Georgia As Interpreted from the Study of Seven Selected Libraries. Master's thesis, Columbia University, 1936.
49 pp., bibl.
The purpose of this study is to relate the significant
steps in the development of libraries in Georgia, with
emphasis on college and university libraries. The author
begins with a brief account of the earliest libraries (before 1800) and then turns to a detailed study of a selected
group of college and university libraries. The seven libraries selected were those at the University of Georgia,
Emory University, Mercer University, Wesleyan College,
Agnes Scott College, Georgia State College for Women,
and Georgia School of Technology. The author discusses
the development of collections, the physical facilities and
the staff. All of the libraries studied suffered from inadequate financial support and were forced to depend
largely on donations in the beginning. It was not until
the turn of the 20th century that separate buildings were
erected, professional librarians appointed, and increased
budgets secured.   251

Illinois

ARCHER, Horace Richard. Some Aspects of the Acquisition Program at the University of Chicago: 1892-1928. Doctoral dissertation, University of Chicago, 1954. 394 pp., bibl. After chronologically tracing the history of the University of Chicago Library 1892-1928, the author gives an account of the development of the Acquisition Department at the University. Emphasis is placed on the various ways in which the library acquired books, such as foreign purchases, gifts, large block acquisitions, and exchanges. 252

HECKMAN, Marlin Leroy. A History of the Library of Bethany Biblical Seminary, Chicago, Illinois. Master's thesis, University of Chicago, 1963. 112 pp., bibl. The author traces the history of library facilities at Bethany from its inception in 1905, at which time the students used the books in the private collection of one of the founders, E. B. Hoff, to the 1960's, when the collection numbered some 44,000 volumes. He analyzes the influence of a number of factors, including the Board of Directors, the administration and faculty, and the standards set by the American Association of Theological Schools. 253

JOHNSON, Elinor Christianna. A History of the Theological Book Collection in the Library of Augustana College and Theological Seminary. Master's thesis, University of Chicago, 1957. 122 pp., bibl. This study traces the development of the library from its beginnings in 1860 up to 1948. The author analyzes the growth of the library in relation to its role as a laboratory for students in theological training. Collection building, physical problems, and faculty influences on library development are some of the factors discussed. 254

McMULLEN, Charles Haynes. The Administration of the University of Chicago Libraries, 1892-1928. Doctoral dissertation, University of Chicago, 1949. 204 pp., bibl. Traces the history of the University of Chicago libraries in terms of administration, with emphasis on collections, staff, financial support, and technical services. Due to faculty insistence the library system was originally made up of a number of autonomous departmental libraries and a general library. Later the University moved toward centralization, but less rapidly than most American universities. Up to 1910 there was no head librarian at the University of Chicago, and after that time the library was headed by faculty members with professional librarians serving as associate librarians. Dr. McMullen found that one of the most serious problems was the lack of uniform cataloging programs, which later forced the library to recatalog its collections. 255

RATCLIFFE, Thomas Edward, Jr. Development of the

Buildings, Policy, Collections of the University of Illinois Library in Urbana. 1897-1940. Master's thesis, University of Illinois, 1949. 111 pp., bibl.
The phases treated are limited to description of the development of the physical plant, the body of regulations and policy, growth of the collection and financial support, and the special collections contained in the library. The paper covers the period from 1897, when Katherine L. Sharp became director, to 1940, when Phineas L. Windsor retired as librarian. 256

WILCOX, Lucile Elizabeth. History of the University of Illinois Library, 1868-1897. Master's thesis, University of Illinois, 1931. 77 pp., bibl.
Surveys the development of the library of the University of Illinois from its beginnings up to 1897, when the library building was erected. The library began with 644 volumes shelved in a recitation room, but was soon large enough to move to rooms in University Hall. By 1897 the collection, which grew quite slowly, contained some 30,000 items. All of the early librarians were from the teaching faculty, and it was not until 1897 that a professional librarian, Miss Katherine Anne Sharpe, was acquired. 257

YENAWINE, Wayne Stewart. The Influence of Scholars on Research Library Development at the University of Illinois. Doctoral dissertation, University of Illinois, 1955. 294 pp., bibl. (D.A. 55-1114).
The University of Illinois Library, one of the finest in the world, took tremendous strides toward its present stature during the period 1900-1930. Dr. Yenawine first investigates the state of scholarship at the University during this era, and then he traces the library's development during the same period. Dr. Yenawine finds that the increased status of scholarship at Illinois and the pressures by scholars for the development of a large research library were instrumental in the library's swift development. At the same time the library was fortunate to have two dynamic and highly respected librarians at the helm during this period: Katherine L. Sharp and Phineas L. Windsor. 258

Indiana

LOWELL, Mildred Hawksworth. Indiana University Libraries, 1829-1942. Doctoral dissertation, University of Chicago, 1957. 453 pp., bibl.
The author considers the development of the Indiana University libraries in terms of the social and economic

forces that directly or indirectly influenced them. Part
one traces the development of the main library from its
beginnings to 1842; part two covers the histories of the
individual branch libraries. The author finds that from
the beginning the library was seen as a vital part of the
University environment. However, its development for
many years was haphazard and few regular appropriations
were made for its upkeep and growth. In the latter part
of the 19th century the library gained regular support, and
its development was accelerated. Planning remained aim-
less, however, and it was not until 1937 that the University administration took deliberate steps to reorganize and
stablize the library system. Numerous Appendices include
lists of librarians and charts of library appropriations. 259

STANLEY, Ellen Lenora. The Earlham College Library; A
History of Its Relation to the College, 1847-1947. Master's thesis, University of Illinois, 1947. 79 pp., bibl.
Earlham College library is analyzed in relation to its
parent institution from its founding in 1847 to 1947. Factors which affected both the college and its library were
examined. They include: (1) government and administration of college; (2) changes in educational theory, curriculum, and emphasis; and (3) the changing size of the
student body.   260

Iowa

SLAVENS, Thomas P. A History of the Drake University Libraries. Master's thesis, University of Minnesota, 1962.
128 pp., bibl.
The author traces the evolution of the Drake University
Library in Des Moines, Iowa, from its beginnings as the
library of Askaloosa College in the early 1860's. In 1881
the institution moved to Des Moines and became Drake
University, but still owned only 13,000 volumes by 1907.
This paper is arranged chronologically according to the
tenure of each of the librarians. The last librarian covered is J. Elias Jones, who took office in 1957, by which
time the collection had grown to nearly 170,000 volumes.   261

Kansas

STEPHENS, H. A Study of the Growth and Development of
the Library of Kansas State Teachers College, Emporia,
1865-1930. Master's thesis, Kansas State Teachers College, 1935. Not examined.   262

BRUNNER, Joyce Estella. The History of the University of
Louisville Libraries. Master's thesis, University of North
Carolina, 1953. 143 pp., bibl. Published: ACRL Microcard #60.
After briefly sketching the history of the University of
Louisville, the author presents individual histories of the
following University of Louisville libraries: (1) the School
of Medicine Library, (2) the School of Law Library, (3)
the General Library, (4) the School of Dentistry Library,
(5) the Speed Scientific School Library, (6) the School of
Music Library, and (7) the Louisville Municipal College
Library. The first library in what is now the University
of Louisville was a small medical library established in
1837.   263

Louisiana

KNIGHTEN, Loma. A History of the Library of Southwestern
Louisiana Institute, 1900-1948. Master's thesis, Columbia
University, 1949. 97 pp., bibl.
This study traces the development of the Library of
Southwestern Louisiana Institute in Lafayette, from the beginning of the college in 1901 to the end of 1948. The
author had three major objectives in mind: (1) to gather
and organize data relating to the library's history, (2) to
show how the growth of the college and changes in the
curricula effected library development, and (3) to show
the library's standing in relation to other state colleges.
The paper includes a brief history of the college, information about the founding of the library, an analysis of
the book collection, a treatment of the growth of staff
and housing, and a history of the administration of the
library.   264

Maine

RUSH, N. Orwin. The History of College Libraries in Maine.
Master's thesis, Columbia University, 1945. 83 pp., bibl.
Published: Clark University Library, Worchester, Mass.,
1946.
This paper is concerned with histories of the libraries of
the five institutions of higher education in Maine. It covers a span of 137 years, from 1802 to 1939. Each library
is treated individually. The author provides information
on origins and development, collection building, use and
function of the libraries, physical facilities, and financial

support. The five schools covered are Bowdoin, Bangor Theological Seminary, Colby, Bates, and the University of Maine. The author finds that church-related groups were influential in establishing most of the schools, and that the library at Bowdoin got the earliest start (1802) and made by far the best progress.   265

Maryland

GREER, James J. A History of the Library of Woodstock College of Baltimore County, Maryland, from 1869 to 1957. Master's thesis, Drexel Institute of Technology, 1957. 84 pp., bibl.
The library of Woodstock College (Jesuit) was founded in 1869. The author devotes his first chapter to a history of the Jesuit scholasticates in Maryland up to 1957. He then discusses the library in a Jesuit house. Chapter III deals with the library of the Georgetown Scholasticate. The final three chapters trace the history of the Woodstock College Library from 1896 to 1957. The author discusses collection development, physical plant, organization of the collection, and services.   266

GRISWOLD, Ardyce Marion. A History of the Columbia Union College Library, Takoma Park, Maryland, 1904-1954. Master's thesis, Catholic University, 1964. 96 pp., bibl.
This study presents a descriptive and statistical survey of the Columbia Union College Library, Takoma Park, Maryland, from its very meagre beginnings in 1904 up to 1954, when it formed a significant part of the Seventh-Day Adventist liberal arts college. The author traces the history of both the college and its library. By 1954 the library's collections numbered nearly 60,000 volumes.   267

HOFF, Alethea. A History of the Library of Western Maryland College. Master's thesis, Drexel Institute of Technology, 1954. 49 pp., bibl.
This study commences with the founding of Western Maryland College in 1867 and traces the development of the library up to 1954. When the college opened in 1867 the only book collection available to students was that owned by Dr. James T. Hall, first president of the school. The library grew slowly and not until 1910 was the first professional librarian appointed. By 1954 the collection had grown to 50,000 volumes, and the library was housed in its own building.   268

KIRBY, Madge Barbour. A History of the Goucher College Library, Baltimore, Maryland, 1885-1949. Master's thesis, Catholic University, 1952. 103 pp., bibl. Published: ACRL Microcard #26.

The Goucher College Library remained quite small for
many years. From 1885 to 1914 the few books were housed in a classroom in Goucher Hall, and faculty members
served as librarians. In 1916 the first full-time librarian
was hired. Library growth was hindered by a number of
factors after 1915, such as the depression of the 30's,
World War II, a split campus, and a general lack of
funds. Despite these difficulties the library grew consistently and was preparing to occupy a new building in 1952.
The contributions of librarian Eleanor N. Falley are considered.   269

KLEIN, Sarah Jannette. The History and Present Status of
the Library of St. John's College, Annapolis. Master's
thesis, Catholic University, 1952. 53 pp., bibl.
The author devotes the first half of her paper to the history of St. John's College and its library. The library
originated in a collection of books sent to Maryland in
1697 by the Rev. Thomas Bray. Many of these books,
which were not enthusiastically received by the colony,
found their way to the St. John's College Library. No organized book purchasing was done by the college library
until 1792, when 275 pounds were expended for books and
other equipment. The collection grew at a snail's pace;
when St. John's College became the Department of Arts
and Sciences of the University of Maryland in 1909 the
library contained only 9,000 volumes. The author briefly
traces the library's development from that time up to
1950.   270

KOUDELKA, Janet B. A History of the Johns Hopkins Medical
Libraries, 1889-1935. Master's thesis, Catholic University, 1963. 96 pp., bibl.
The author divides her study into three major portions.
The first deals with the early medical libraries at Johns
Hopkins: the hospital library, 1889-1929; the library of
the School of Medicine, 1893-1929; and the library of the
School of Hygiene and Public Health, 1919-1929. The
second portion traces the developments that led to the
establishment of a centralized medical library, the William W. Welch Medical Library, in 1929. The third portion treats the Welch Medical Library under the directorship of Fielding H. Garrison, 1930-1934.   271

LUCKETT, George Ridgely. A History of the United States
Naval Academy Library, 1845-1907. Master's thesis,
Catholic University, 1951. 39 pp., bibl.
This paper traces the history of the United States Naval
Academy Library from its beginnings in 1845, when it
was a small collection of about 300 volumes to 1904,
when the collection had grown to nearly 50,000 volumes.

Although the library's development parallels somewhat
the histories of other American libraries of the 19th century, the author feels that its history is more closely
connected with the history of the United States. The United
States Naval Academy and its library prospered when the
Navy was popular and declined when the people lost interest in the Navy. Thus the library grew rapidly during
such periods as the 1860's, late 1880's and early 90's
and in the period of glory after the Spanish American
War.   272
NICHOLS, M. E. Historical Survey of the Library of the Col-
    lege of Notre Dame of Maryland. Master's thesis, Cath-
    olic University, 1957. 83 pp., Not examined.   273
OWINGS, Vivian Briggs. A History of the Library of Morgan
    State College from 1867 to 1939. Master's thesis, Cath-
    olic University, 1952. 32 pp., bibl.
    Morgan State College, in Baltimore, Maryland, began in
    1867 as the Centenary Biblical Institute. It was one of
    the many educational endeavors aimed at the newly emanci-
    pated American Negro. The first library collection avail-
    able to students was the private holdings of Dr. J. Emory
    Round, first president of the Centenary Institute. It was
    not until 1920 that any extensive library development took
    place, stimulated by a grant from the Carnegie Founda-
    tion and the appointment of the first professional librar-
    ian at the college. The author surveys book budgets,
    staff development, physical plant, and services for the
    period 1867-1939.   274
RODDY, Sister Ruth. A History of Saint Joseph College Li-
    brary, 1902-1955. Emmitsburg, Maryland. Master's the-
    sis, Catholic University, 1956. 103 pp., bibl.
    The author has written her history of the Saint Joseph
    College library from 1902-1953 under the following major
    headings: (1) a brief history of the college, (2) housing,
    (3) finances, (4) growth and development of the book and
    periodical collections, (5) administration, (6) staffing, and
    (7) organization of the collection. Saint Joseph's gained
    authorization to function as a college in 1902 and from
    that time on the college had a library, although it re-
    mained quite small. In 1955 the budget was only $5,000
    and the collection numbered 20,000 volumes.   275

Massachusetts

ENGLEY, Donald B. The Emergence of the Amherst College
    Library, 1821-1911. Master's thesis, University of Chi-
    cago, 1947. 155 pp., bibl.
    The Amherst College library progressed slowly at first.

Faced by a shortage of funds and a seemingly disinterested attitude on the part of the faculty, little progress was made before 1845. Under the energetic guidance of President Edward Hitchcock the first library building was provided in 1853. An increased faculty and student interest, plus increased appropriations, soon put a strain on the library's cramped quarters. In the 1870's Melvil Dewey spent a short time at Amherst and developed the beginnings of his classification scheme. However, the great growth of the library took place under the leadership of one of America's leading 19th-century librarians, William I. Fletcher, who served the Amherst Library from 1883 to 1911. Appendices include abstracts of the catalogs issued during the period covered.   276

TERRELL, Darrell. History of the Dumberton Oaks Research Library of Harvard University, 1940-1950. Master's thesis, Catholic University, 1954. 51 pp., bibl.
Traces the history of the Dumberton Oaks Research Library at Harvard, which is devoted to the study of Byzantine history and culture. The first chapter discusses the early development of the library by its founders, Mr. and Mrs. Robert Woods Elise. In 1940 the library building, the collection of some 14,000 books, and 16 acres of land (the whole gift valued at over $1,000,000) were given to Harvard University. Chapter two deals with the library's development after 1940, with special emphasis on administration, services, and the collection. Chapter three deals with special collections and reference tools developed at the library.   277

Michigan

BIDLACK, Russell Eugene. The University of Michigan General Library: A History of Its Beginnings, 1837-1852. Doctoral dissertation, University of Michigan, 1954. 663 pp., bibl. (D.A. 54-1588).
This study covers the history of the library, which had its inception together with the University in 1837. The Rev. Henry Colelazer, a local clergyman, was the first librarian. He served in that capacity until 1845, at which time he was replaced by Professor George P. Williams. Williams worked up a classification for the collection adapted from Thomas Jefferson's plan, and he printed a catalog in 1846. Three early catalogs form the Appendices of Dr. Bidlack's study.   278

Minnesota

FORTIN, Charles C. A History of the St. Thomas College Library. Master's thesis, University of Minnesota, 1951. 187 pp., bibl.

The author first traces the history of St. Thomas College in St. Paul, Minnesota. A library was available when the college opened as St. Thomas Aquinas Seminary in 1885, but little is known about it until 1918, when Miss Mary Griffin was named the first full-time librarian. The author divides his history of the library into chronological segments corresponding to the tenure of the librarians: Mary Griffin (1918-1926), Bonita McElmeel (1926-1931), Blaise Hospodor (1931-1932), Leonard Pogge (1932-1937), Bernadette Becker (1937-1944) and David Watkins (1944-to time of study). The author finds that the library was plagued from the beginning by the difficulties in preparing a catalog and the problems relating to physical facilities for the library.   279

MILLER, Virginia P. A History of the Library of Gustavus Adolphus College, St. Peter, Minnesota. Master's thesis, University of Minnesota, 1961. 192 pp., bibl.

This paper first presents a chronological history of the development of the library at Gustavus Adolphus College from its beginnings in 1862 until the summer of 1960. The library was managed for some 60 years by faculty librarians, and the author gives extensive coverage to their contributions to library development. The first professionally trained librarian was appointed in the 20's. The rest of the paper is developed around the three librarians who served from 1919 to 1960: Mrs. Victoria Johnston (1919-1943), Grant D. Hanson (1945-1950), and Miss Odrun Peterson (1950 to present). The library was moved to a new building in 1948 and in 1960 contained more than 65,000 volumes.   280

ROLOFF, Ronald William. St. John's University Library: A Historical Evaluation. Master's thesis, University of Minnesota, 1953. 319 pp., bibl. Published: ACRL Microcard #34.

Traces the evolution of the St. John's University Library in Collegeville, Minnesota, from its earliest beginnings in 1867 up to 1953. The library grew out of a small and secluded collection of books, overwhelmingly theological in content. By 1950 the library had grown to 80,000 volumes, but was still plagued by a lack of funds and space.   281

Mississippi

NICHOLS, Mary Elizabeth. Early Development of the University

of Mississippi Library. Master's thesis, University of Mississippi, 1957. 50 pp., bibl. Published: ACRL Microcard #111.
This study traces the history of the University of Mississippi Library from 1849 to 1910. The first years of the University's history were characterized by exteme financial difficulties and the library suffered accordingly. The first librarian, a faculty member, was named in 1853, but it was not until 1886 that a full-time librarian was appointed. The library was damaged during the Civil War and lay dormant during the turbulent Reconstruction period. The library reached a period of relatively smooth growth by 1910.   282

Missouri

HOYER, Mina. The History of Automation in the University of Missouri Library, 1947-1963. Master's thesis, Indiana University, 1965. 74 pp., bibl. Published: ACRL Microcard #166.
This paper traces the history of automation at the University of Missouri from 1947, when Dr. Ralph Parker became librarian, to 1963. Dr. Parker has been a pioneer in library automation, and the author analyzes his efforts in this area. Steps in planning, changes made, and current (1965) planning for future development are discussed. The author has not attempted to theorize about all possible types of library machines, but treats only those that are being used or that seem best fitted to future application at the University of Missouri Library.   283

New York

BOGART, Ruth E. College Library Development in New York State During the 19th Century. Master's thesis, Columbia, 1948. 155 pp., bibl.
The author presents a history of the development of college libraries in New York during the 19th century. She treats her subject topically and covers the following major areas: (1) early provisions for college libraries, (2) methods of expanding libraries, (3) growth of the collections, (4) restrictions on acquisitions, (5) housing, (6) library organization, and (7) library instruction. The author finds that religion had some influence on college libraries in New York, though less extensive than in the 1700's. The Civil War did not cause serious problems for college libraries in New York. The American Library Association, established in 1876, was most stimulating to the older college libraries of the state.   284

JONES, Ruth. A History of the Library of Teachers College, Columbia University, 1887-1952. Master's thesis, Drexel Institute of Technology, 1953. 35 pp., bibl. Published: ACRL Microcard #39.

After briefly tracing the history of Columbia Teachers College, the author covers the history of the library in three time periods. The library got a tremendous boost when Columbia College transferred over 20,000 volumes on education to the Bryson Library at the Teachers College in 1903. By 1952 the collection, which had numbered 500 volumes in 1888, had grown to over 250,000. 285

KATO, Mother Ayako. A History of Brady Memorial Library, Manhattanville College of the Sacred Heart; Purchase, New York, 1841-1957. Master's thesis, Catholic University, 1959. 143 pp., bibl.

The author has concentrated on the history of the library of Manhattanville College, a small Catholic liberal arts college for women, but she has also made a serious effort to contrast this library's development with others in America. Special emphasis is placed on tracing the active influence the library has exerted on the educational role of Manhattanville College. The author follows a topical arrangement concerned with five major subjects: physical plant, administration, the book collection, technical services, and public services. 286

LINDERMAN, Winifred B. History of the Columbia University Library, 1876-1926. Doctoral dissertation, Columbia University, 1959. 619 pp., bibl. (D.A. 59-2859)

Though King's College was established in 1754, the author has chosen to cover the years 1876-1926 in her study because these years saw its transition from college to major university and the concomitant evolution of the library from a small collection of books to one of the largest research facilities in America. Dr. Linderman considers the many difficulties involved in this transition--such matters as collection building, personnel problems, administrative practices and physical plant planning. The librarians of Columbia were among the most significant of their day. Melvil Dewey established the country's first library school, to train assistants for the Columbia University Library. George H. Baker, Dewey's successor, was noted for his collection building efforts. In 1926 the noted library educator and administrator, Dr. Charles C. Williamson, was named Director of Libraries and Dean of the School of Library Service. 287

North Carolina

BATTLE, Margaret Elizabeth. A History of the Carnegie Library at Johnson C. Smith University. Master's thesis, University of North Carolina, 1960. 55 pp., bibl.
This study traces the development of the Carnegie Library at Johnson C. Smith University, a Negro college in Charlotte, North Carolina, from the latter part of the 19th century to 1958. At first the library was simply a collection of books in one of the classrooms. By 1890 it had reached nearly 5,000 volumes, most of them theological in nature. In 1903 Andrew Carnegie offered to donate $12,500 for a library building if the University could match this amount for upkeep. The University managed by 1911 to raise the money. In 1958 the collection numbered some 30,000 volumes. The author devotes one chapter to the development of the theological library at the University.   288

CLYMER, Benjamin Franklin, Jr. The History of the Division of Health Affairs Library of the University of North Carolina, Master's thesis, University of North Carolina, 1959. 118 pp., bibl.
The origins of the Division of Health Affairs Library are traced back to 1800, to the book collections of the University and the libraries of its two literary societies. The collections contained few medical books, and those few were obsolete gifts. In 1912 the collection, some 3,000 outdated volumes, was housed in a "library room" in the medical building. The collection grew slowly and spasmodically due to a lack of funds. In 1936, the collection was made a departmental library of the University Library and from that time on took on some semblance of organized growth. By 1959 the library had grown to nearly 70,000 volumes and had a staff of four.   289

CRANFORD, Janet Parrish. The Documents Collection of the University of North Carolina Library from Its Beginnings Through 1963. Master's thesis, University of North Carolina, 1965. Not examined.   290

DIAZ, Albert James. A History of the Latin American Collection of the University of North Carolina Library. Master's thesis, University of North Carolina, 1956. 83 pp., bibl.
This paper is divided into three main sections. The first deals with the historical development of the collection. Up to 1940 the growth of the collection was irregular, hampered by a lack of funds. From 1940 to 1945 the collection was greatly increased with $25,000 provided by the Rockefeller Foundation. In 1947 the Carnegie Corporation provided $14,000 over a five-year period to be used in building up the holdings. In 1952 the library had grown

to 20,000 volumes and from that time on was financed
wholly by the University. Part two deals with the problems
faced in acquiring and processing the collection. Part
three is a critical evaluation of the development of the
collection.   291
EATON, Joan Davis. A History and Evaluation of the Hanes
    Collection in the Louis R. Wilson Library, University of
    North Carolina. Master's thesis, University of North
    Carolina, 1957. 115 pp., bibl.
    This paper traces the history of the Hanes collection from
    the time of Louis Round Wilson's first conception of it
    until 1957. Dr. Wilson had long hoped to establish a spe-
    cial collection of materials relating to the history of books
    and bookmaking, but it was not until 1929 that his plans
    bore fruit. At that time the Hanes Foundation for the
    study of the origin and development of the book was es-
    tablished by the children of John Wesley and Anna Hodgin
    Hanes. Thirty thousand dollars was given to the Univer-
    sity, $20,000 of which was to be spent for the purchase
    of 369 incunabula owned by Dr. Aaron Burtis Hunter of
    Raleigh. Since that time, and especially since 1951, the
    collection has grown steadily and now stands as one of
    the best of its kind in the South.   292
FARROW, Mildred Hayward. The History of Guilford College
    Library, 1837-1955. Master's thesis, University of North
    Carolina, 1959. 164 pp., tables, bibl. Published: ACRL
    Microcard #120.
    The history of the Guilford College Library, Greensboro,
    North Carolina, is closely linked with the efforts of the
    North Carolina Society of Friends to provide books for
    meeting libraries in the 1830's. The Friends presented
    the library with many gifts and by 1886 the collection
    numbered over 20,000 volumes. The library was destroy-
    ed by fire in 1908, but was quickly rebuilt and with the
    help of a Carnegie grant was able to acquire over 20,000
    volumes by 1950.   293
HOLDER, Elizabeth Jerome. A History of the Library of the
    Woman's College of the University of North Carolina,
    1892-1945. Master's thesis, University of North Carolina,
    1955. 144 pp., bibl. Published: ACRL Microcard #86.
    After briefly tracing the history of the school founded in
    1891 in Greensboro, North Carolina, the author presents
    the history of the library from its inception in 1892 to
    1945. Chapters are devoted to: (1) the general history of
    the library, (2) the influence of Carnegie funds on library
    development, (3) the Department of Library Science, 1927-
    1931, (4) special collections and gifts; (5) periodical col-
    lections, and (6) the library fire of 1932.   294

LIST, Barbara Turner. The Friends of the University of North Carolina Library, 1932-1962. Master's thesis, University of North Carolina, 1965. 65 pp., bibl.

The first section of this paper contains a history of the rise of "Friends of the Library" throughout the United States. The first of these groups was founded in 1923. The author then turns her attention to the Friends of the University of North Carolina, which developed under the guidance of the noted librarian Louis R. Wilson. The author finds that the group has had a significant influence on the library's development. Such things as the purchase of special collections, lobbying for new buildings or larger budgets, and general support of the library's programs are cited.   295

MOORE, Gay Garrison. The Southern Historical Collection in the Louis Round Wilson Library of the University of North Carolina from the Beginning of the Collection Through 1948. Master's thesis, University of North Carolina, 1958. 83 pp., bibl.

The Southern Historical Collection includes all of the relevant manuscript holdings of the University Library at Chapel Hill. The collection was developed through the efforts of Dr. Joseph Gregoine de Roulhac Hamilton, who was one of the first to realize the services needed for a large, well organized collection of manuscript material on Southern history. The collection was formally recognized in 1930 and Dr. Hamilton was named director. By 1943, when he retired, the collection was considered one of the best in the United States.   296

NICHOLSON, James M., Jr. A History of the Wake Forest College Library, 1878-1946. Master's thesis, University of North Carolina, 1954. 105 pp., bibl. Published: ACRL Microcard #78.

The chapters of this paper deal with the following subjects: (1) the introduction of "New Education" methods into American education and their effect on Wake Forest College before 1900; (2) the library during the period of transition from the controlling influence of the classical curriculum to the equivalent status of "New Education" courses, 1879-1905; (3) the library during the administration of William L. Poteat, 1905-1927; and (4) the library and two benefactors - Andrew Carnegie and E. Smith Reynolds, 1928-1946.   297

PEARSALL, Thelma F. History of the North Carolina Agricultural and Technical College Library. Master's thesis, Western Reserve, 1955. 48 pp., bibl.

After surveying the development of Greensboro, North Carolina, and its college, the author divides the history

of the library into four sections: (1) the librarians, from
Ferdinand D. Bluford in 1912 to Miss Morrow (1937-);
(2) the library buildings, including the old library that
was destroyed in 1929, the new quarters provided in 1931,
and the new building erected in 1954; (3) the library's
collections; and (4) library services.   298

PERKINS, Theodore Edison. The History of Elon College Library, 1890-1957. Master's thesis, University of North
Carolina, 1962. 148 pp. , bibl.
This study presents the history 1890-1957, of the library
of Elon College, located in Elon, North Carolina. The
author divides his topic into seven basic parts. The first
part consists of a brief history of the Christian Church
(Congregational Christian) from which the college sprang,
and a brief history of the college itself. Part two deals
with the early history of the library and its numerous
difficulties. The third part deals with the library's staff.
The fourth part analyzes the development of the library's
services. The fifth part analyzes the development of the
library's collection. Part six deals with cataloging and
classification, and part seven describes the use made of
the Elon College Library during the period covered. 299

Ohio

BOBINSKI, George S. A Brief History of the Libraries of
Western Reserve University, 1826-1952. Master's thesis,
Western Reserve, 1952. 77 pp. , bibl.
The author describes the evolution of the Western Reserve University Library from a collection of 100 volumes in 1826 to some 700,000 in 1952. The continuous
efforts to meet ever-increasing demands for space and
the need for unifying the library system are the two major themes in the paper. A major portion of the paper
treats the development of the Adelbert College Library of
the University from 1882 to 1924.   300

BROOKOVER, Barbara. A History of the Leonard Case Library, Cleveland, Ohio, 1846-1941. Master's thesis,
Western Reserve, 1957. 37 pp. , bibl.
Few libraries have had so varied a history as the Case
Library. It traces its beginning to the establishment of
the Young Men's Literary Association in 1846. In 1867
it moved to the new library rooms of the Cleveland Library Association, founded and paid for by Leonard Case
in memory of his brother William. The library continued
to develop with the aid of Mr. Case for many years. In
1924 the library merged with Western Reserve University
and Adelbert College.   301

CLINEFELLER, Ruth W. A History of Bierce Library of the University of Akron. Master's thesis, Kent State University, 1956. 200 pp., bibl.

This paper traces the history of the library, which began as part of Buchtel College, from 1872 to 1955. Library development was slow, especially after the financial crisis of 1893. In 1916 a new library was built and the collection began to expand. In 1949 a special library on rubber was established with funds from the Rubber Division of the American Chemical Society. By 1955 the Bierce Library held 100,000 volumes.   302

IRWIN, Maurine. History of the Ohio Wesleyan University Library, 1844-1940. Master's thesis, University of California, 1941. 263 pp., bibl.

The library developed slowly until William Starges donated $10,000 in 1853 to increase the collection. This enabled the University to purchase a nucleus of some 3,000 volumes for the library--a collection that was slowly enlarged as was the case with most college libraries. The Ohio Wesleyan University Library had an irregular and insufficient budget. Most acquisitions came through gifts. In the 20th century the library developed along more organized lines, but was still hampered by serious financial difficulties in 1940.   303

MEYERS, Judith K. A History of the Antioch College Library, 1850-1929. Master's thesis, Kent State University, 1963. 166 pp., bibl. Published: ACRL Microcard #150.

Studies the history of the Antioch College Library, Yellow Springs, Ohio, in relation to broad social, political, economic and cultural currents of the times. This study covers the library's history from its founding up to 1920. The author finds that significant shortages of money, space, and personnel hampered the growth of the library. By 1920 the library contained about 30,000 volumes. 304

SAVIERS, Samuel H. The Literary Societies and Their Libraries at Hiram College. Master's thesis, Kent State University, 1958. 277 pp., bibl.

This paper is developed in three parts: (1) the history of the literary societies of Hiram College (1850-1950); (2) their purposes, organization, and activities; and (3) their libraries. The libraries are studied in depth and their contributions to Hiram College are analyzed. In the 19th century the society libraries arose as a result of the inadequacy of the college library, and the author finds their contributions to the college library exceedingly important.   305

SCHINK, Ronald John. A History of the Youngstown University and Its Library. Master's thesis, Western Reserve, 1956.

65 pp., bibl.

This study is mainly concerned with a history of the University. The latter portion of the paper does trace in some detail the development of the library from 1937 to 1950. In 1943 the school was refused accreditation because the library facilities were inadequate. The library made considerable progress after 1943; the author traces its development with emphasis on the events surrounding the construction of the new library in 1950-1951.   306

SILVA, Sister M. Frances Clane. A History of the Ursuline College Library, Cleveland, Ohio, 1922-1957. Master's thesis, Western Reserve, 1958. 49 pp., bibl. Published: ACRL Microcard #108.

Briefly covers the history of Ursuline College and then discusses the library's history from its beginnings in 1922 up to 1957. The treatment is chronological with special consideration given to budget, collection, buildings, organization and services. By 1957 the library contained more than 20,000 volumes.   307

SKIPPER, James Everett. The Ohio State University Library, 1873-1913. Doctoral dissertation, University of Michigan, 1960. 330 pp., bibl. (D.A. 60-6937).

Part one of Dr. Skipper's study considers the problems of the physical plant, faculty-library relations, and development of the library's collections from 1873-1893. Part two deals with the history of the library from 1893 until 1913, when the first permanent library building was completed. During the whole 40-year period covered, the growth of the University library was restricted by a lack of legislative support.   308

STEIN, John H. The Development of the Hiram College Library from the Literary Societies Which Formed Its Nucleus. Master's thesis, Kent State University, 1950. 105 pp., bibl.

Traces the history of the Hiram College Library, Hiram, Ohio, from the beginnings of the literary society libraries in the 1850's up to 1940. The author places special emphasis on the factors influencing acquisition policies in the college library. The literary society libraries were found to be the only good libraries on campus until after 1900, and they proved vital to the academic program of the University.   309

TUCKER, Jennie Streeter. Oberlin College Library, 1833-1885. Master's thesis, Western Reserve, 1953. 125 pp., bibl.

The Oberlin College Library experienced its greatest growth after 1885, but the author has chosen its early period for the subject of this paper. The library got official recognition in 1834, and for the next 40 years it was under the able direction of Dr. James Dascomb, Professor of Chemistry, Physiology and Botany. The author found ledgers recording the books checked out to students in 1836 and presents a list of the titles. A number of literary society libraries were established and they too are discussed. 310

VERMILYA, Nancy C. A History of the Otterbein College Library. Master's thesis, Western Reserve, 1955. 49 pp., bibl. Published: ACRL Microcard #58.
Traces the history of the Otterbein College Library, Westerville, Ohio, from its inception in 1858 to 1955. The paper is divided into two parts: (1) the history of the literary societies and their four libraries at Otterbein; and (2) history of the development of the college library in its five locations. In 1955 the new library building held nearly 50,000 volumes. 311

Pennsylvania

CUNNING, Ellen T. A History of Jefferson Medical College Library, 1898-1953. Master's thesis, Drexel Institute of Technology, 1954. 36 pp., bibl.
This study begins with a brief history of the Medical College, which was first established in 1825. Then the author writes a history of the College's library. In 1898 the Women's Auxiliary of the Jefferson Medical College of Philadelphia was formed and began work that led to the establishment of a reading room for the students of that college. In 1906 a new library building was built with part of a $1,250,000 gift by Samuel Parsons Scott. The author traces the development of the collection, services and physical plant to 1953. 312

EARNSHAW, Jeannine. A History of the Henry Lea Library at the University of Pennsylvania. Master's thesis, Drexel Institute of Technology, 1955. 41 pp., bibl.
This study emphasizes the growth of the collection and stresses its importance as a center for historical research. Henry Lea was a Philadelphia scholar interested in medieval law. He collected a remarkable library while doing his research. A survey of his collection in 1878 showed that he owned over 15,000 books and an impressive collection of manuscripts. It soon became, and remained, one of the best collections on the Inquisition, medieval jurisprudence, and the ecclesiastical courts. Upon his death he left his library to the University of Pennsylvania; in 1925 a new wing was added to the University's main library to hold the collection. The author devotes the final

two chapters to a discussion of the administration of the library and the development of its collections.   313

GIRVIN, Anne Gabrief. The Albright Alumni Memorial Library. Master's thesis, Drexel Institute of Technology, 1954. 65 pp. , bibl.
This paper surveys the history of the Albright Alumni Memorial Library, located in Albright College, Reading, Pennsylvania. The library at Albright College had as its nucleus the collections of three earlier colleges: the Union Seminary, Schuylkill College, and Albright Collegiate Institution. This study covers the history of these libraries chronologically from 1853 to 1953, dealing with the early history of the institutions, with the libraries of the three background institutions, and finally with the Albright College Library to 1953.   314

McFARLAND, M. M. History of the Development of Bucknell University Library, Lewisburg, Pennsylvania. Master's thesis, Drexel Institute of Technology, 1955. Not examined.   315

McTAGGART, John Barney. The History of the Eastern Baptist Theological Seminary Library, 1925-1953. Master's thesis, Drexel Institute of Technology, 1954. 63 pp. , bibl.
This paper traces the historical development of the Eastern Baptist Theological Seminary Library, Philadelphia, Pennsylvania, from its beginning in 1925 until 1953. The study does not attempt a critical analysis of the library and its holdings are not covered in detail. Emphasis has been placed on the library's physical facilities, and staff, rather than on its services.   316

MEYEREND, Maude H. A History and Survey of the Fine Arts Library of the University of Pennsylvania from Its Founding to 1953. Master's thesis, Drexel Institute of Technology, 1955. 92 pp. , bibl.
The first part of this paper sketches the history of the Fine Arts Department and its library at the University of Pennsylvania from 1906 to 1953. The rest of the paper is devoted to a survey of present conditions (1955).   317

OSBORNE, John T. The Ursinus College Library, 1869-1953. Master's thesis, Drexel Institute of Technology, 1954. 44 pp. , bibl.
Presents the history of the Ursinus College Library, Collegeville, Pennsylvania, from the founding of the College in 1869 until the end of 1953. The first chapter covers the history of the college, the next three chapters cover the development of the library, and a final chapter discusses the construction of the Alumni Memorial Library Building.   318

RICHARDSON, Ellen R. The La Salle College Library, Philadelphia, 1930-1953. Master's thesis, Drexel Institute of

116

Technology, 1953. 43 pp., bibl.

This study traces the growth of the library from 1930 to 1953, with special emphasis on the plans for the new building and its occupancy. From the beginning the collection was small and poorly housed. The first librarian bought his make-shift book shelves at a local hardware store and installed them himself. The lack of an adequate budget limited the library's development. In 1950 the college administration agreed to spend $400,000 on a new main library building. The author traces the development of the plans for this building and describes the steps taken to occupy it.   319

SEVY, Barbara. Temple University School of Medicine Library, 1910-1954. Master's thesis, Drexel Institute of Technology, 1955. 61 pp., bibl.

This study is divided into five sections: (1) a history of the Temple College Library from 1892-1900; (2) a history of the Medical School and the Medical Library, 1921-1929; (3) the library of the professional schools (Dentistry, Medicine, and Pharmacy), 1921-1929; (4) the Samaritan Hospital Library, 1929-1930; and (5) the School of Medicine Library, 1930-1954.   320

SMITH, Dorothy Jeanne. The Early History of the Library of Allegheny College, Meadville, Pennsylvania. Master's thesis, Western Reserve, 1953. 58 pp., bibl. Published: ACRL Microcard #61.

In 1815, and for several years thereafter, the library was the only asset of the new college. Timothy Alden, founder and first president of the college, was an ardent book collector and solicited gifts from such noted New Englanders as John Adams, William Bentley, Isaiah Thomas, and James Winthrop. The author discusses these benefactions and others, the development of the physical plant, the production of the catalog of 1823, and concludes with the year 1837.   321

WAGNER, Lloyd F. A Descriptive History of the Library Facilities of Lafayette College, Easton, Pennsylvania, 1826-1941. Master's thesis, Catholic University, 1951. 91 pp., bibl. Published: ACRL Microcard #27.

This paper is a descriptive and statistical study covering the following subjects: (1) the effect of Lafayette College and library administrators, and especially of the students, on library development; (2) the development of library facilities, financial support, and services; (3) the influence of student literary societies at Lafayette College from 1832 to 1900; (4) the increasing significance of the library to the educational programs; and (5) a comparison of the Lafayette College Library with others of similar size,

Tennessee

ATKINS, E. History of the Fisk University Library and Its
  Standing in Relation to the Libraries of Other Comparable
  Institutions. Master's thesis, University of California,
  1936. 83 pp., Not examined.   323
DUNCAN, Ruth Batterton. A History of the George Peabody
  College Library, 1785-1910. Master's thesis, George Peabody, 1940. 95 pp., bibl.
  The author presents a history of the George Peabody College Library from its beginnings in 1785 to 1910. Its major purpose is to describe, analyze and evaluate the state
  of the library in the colleges (Davidson Academy, Cumber-
  land College, Nashville University) that evolved into the
  George Peabody College.   324

Texas

COCHRAN, Mary Akin. The University of Texas Package Loan
  Library, 1914-1954. Master's thesis, University of Texas,
  1956. 206 pp., bibl.
  Prior to 1914 the loan of packages of debate materials
  was part of the extension services of the University of
  Texas. In 1914 this service was taken over by a new
  package loan library, patterned after one at the University
  of Wisconsin. Besides supporting the University extension
  courses, the package loan library assumed the responsibility of providing information on current subjects to all
  of the citizens of Texas. The author describes the development of the package loan library and then surveys its
  current condition (1954).   325
LEE, Joe Bill. A History of the Library of Texas College of
  Arts and Industries, 1925-1955. Master's thesis, University of Texas, 1958. 148 pp., bibl.
  This is a history of the library of the Texas College of
  Arts and Industries, in Kingsville, Texas, from 1925 to
  1955. It emphasizes the development of the library's
  resources--financial, staff, collections, and physical plant.
  Little attention is paid to such aspects as government,
  reader services, and the use of the library. The author
  points out that his emphasis is on the latter part of the
  period 1925-1955 because of a lack of materials relating
  to earlier years. Mr. Lee makes extensive use of tabular
  displays to conserve space and present detailed information.   326
ROUSE, Roscoe, Jr. A History of the Baylor University

Library, 1845-1919. Doctoral dissertation, University of
Michigan, 1962. 390 pp., bibl.
The author presents a study of the development of an academic library on the frontier. He traces chronologically
the development of the library from its inception to the
retirement of librarian Willard P. Lewis in 1919, at which
time the library was viewed as an established service institution in the University. Dr. Rouse gives the history
of libraries within Baylor University literary and debating
societies. The librarians of the University, the first appointed in 1888, are considered in the light of their contributions to the university and their profession. The development of the physical plant at the library is covered
with special emphasis on the events surrounding the gift
of the F. L. Carroll Chapel and Library in 1901.   327

Virginia

EDSALL, Margaret Harriman. History of the Library of the
Protestant Episcopal Theological Seminary in Virginia,
1823-1955. Master's thesis, Catholic University, 1955.
66 pp., bibl.
The author begins this history with a brief survey of the
seminary and then traces the history of the seminary's
library from 1823 to 1955. This study emphasizes the
positive role enlightened giving can play in building the
book collection of a library with a very small book budget. By 1955 the collection had grown to 40,000--many of
them gifts.   328
HUDSON, Jeanne Perry. A History of the Roanoke College Library, 1842-1959. Master's thesis, University of North
Carolina, 1963. 80 pp., bibl.
The author presents the 117-year history of the library of
Roanoke College and analyzes certain trends and influences. The paper is arranged chronologically under four major headings: (1) Founding of the Library; (2) The New Building; (3) The Library Comes of Age; and (4) Continued
Growth. The author found that the college library suffered considerably from a lack of sound financial backing,
but made extensive progress due to the continuous support
of the college's presidents.   329

Washington

POTTER, Jessica Chandler. The History of the University of
Washington Library. Master's thesis, University of Washington, 1954. 107 pp., bibl. Published: ACRL Microcard
#56.

Presents a history of the University of Washington Library
from its small beginning in 1862, as part of the Territorial University, up to 1950. The arrangement is chronological, except for two chapters dealing with coordination
of the library system and cooperation with other libraries.
The library's relationship with the School of Librarianship
is not covered.   330

West Virginia

AMOS, Autumn. A History of the Robert F. Kidd Library.
Master's thesis, Western Reserve, 1953. 45 pp., bibl.
The author describes the development of the library at
Glenville State College, Glenville, West Virginia, from
1879 to 1952. His topics are (1) the librarians, with emphasis on librarian Alma Janet Arbuckle; (2) the library
buildings, with emphasis on the Kidd Library built in 1930;
and (3) the book collection.   331

HARRIS, Virgie. Library Development in Five Denominational
Colleges in West Virginia. Master's thesis, Western Reserve, 1952. 106 pp., bibl.
The five college libraries studied are those of Bethany College, Salem College, West Virginia Wesleyan College, Al-
derson-Broaddus College, and Davis and Elkins College.
This study covers the period 1842-1952; emphasis, due to
a lack of early records, is on the 20th century. The author studies the relationship of the initial or early book
collections to the role of the college, then compares the
development of the libraries in terms of holdings, staff,
budgets, and circulation. Several of the early collections
were owned by literary societies and the author traces
their transition from society library to college library. 332

MUNN, Robert Ferguson. West Virginia University Library,
1867-1917. Doctoral dissertation, University of Michigan,
1962. 260 pp., bibl.
Dr. Munn considers the development of this library in the
total context of the University's evolution. The opening
parts of the work contain a survey of social and economic
conditions in West Virginia, plus a detailed examination
of the developmental history of the University. After providing this background data the author launches into the
history of the library. Like most university libraries it
encountered considerable difficulties from the start. Housed
in small and poorly suited quarters, run by a professor-
librarian who devoted only a minimum of time to his library duties, and plagued by a shortage of funds (only
$7,223 was spent for books from 1868-1885), the library
developed slowly until 1897. At that time Jerome H.

Raymond, an ardent believer in good libraries, was named president of the University. He hired the University's first professional librarian, Miss Eliza J. Skinner, and he was successful in increasing library appropriations and in obtaining a new building. The author concludes by comparing the Library of West Virginia University with those of other state-supported universities in Georgia, Kentucky, North Carolina, Tennessee and Virginia. 333

Wisconsin

HUBBARD, Corinne. History of Wisconsin State College, Oshkosh, Library, September, 1871-August, 1943. Master's thesis, Drexel Institute of Technology, 1954. 69 pp., bibl. The author begins her paper with a brief survey of the Wisconsin State College in Oshkosh, which was founded in 1871. She then traces the history of the college's library from its inception in 1871 up to 1953. At first the collection was small, with students and faculty taxing themselves to provide funds for the library's program. The library grew quite rapidly, due mainly to a number of large gifts, but most of it was lost in a fire in 1916. By 1953 the collection had been rebuilt to nearly 50,000 volumes and was housed in a new building. The author divides her paper into four major sections: (1) Housing of the library; (2) The collection; (3) Library science classes; and (4) The librarians. 334

KRUEGER, Hanna Elsa. History of the Carroll College Library. Master's thesis, University of Chicago, 1943. 164 pp., bibl.
This study begins with a history of Carroll College of Waukesha, Wisconsin from 1846 to 1942. The author then traces the history of the library 1851-1942. The founders of Carroll College recognized the need for library facilities from the beginning; however, few funds were appropriated for collection building until after 1900. Up to that time the only source of incoming books was gifts. Not until 1911 was a full-time librarian appointed, and it was not until 1926 that the first professionally-trained librarian was named. Appendix A includes a chronological table of important dates in the history of the college and of the library. 335

Special Libraries

Business and Industrial Libraries.

BROWN, James Vincent. History of the Industrial Relations

Research Libraries. Master's thesis, Western Reserve, 1958. 87 pp., bibl.
This paper presents short histories of the industrial relations libraries at the United States Department of Labor, Princeton, University of Michigan, Stanford, Massachusetts Institute of Technology, California Institute of Technology, Loyola, Harvard, St. Joseph's College, Yale, University of Denver, Cornell, University of Chicago, University of California, LeMoyne College, University of Minnesota, University of Illinois, University of Washington, San Jose State, Michigan State, University of Wisconsin, Rutgers, University of Hawaii, and State University of Iowa.
A final chapter is a chronological outline of the activities of the Committee of University Industrial Relations Librarians.   336

HARRIS, Jeanette F. The Newspaper Library: Its History, Function, and Value with Special Reference to the New York Herald Tribune. Master's thesis, Southern Connecticut, 1959. 46 pp., bibl.
The author devotes the first 20 pages of this paper to the history of the newspaper library of the New York Herald, which later merged with the New York Tribune to become the New York Herald Tribune. Emphasis is placed on the special problems encountered by the librarians of a large metropolitan newspaper.   337

KRUZAS, Anthony Thomas. The Development of Special Libraries for American Business and Industry. Doctoral dissertation, University of Michigan, 1960. 367 pp., bibl. Published: Special Libraries Association, 1965.
Dr. Kruzas based his research on the analysis of data contained in ten special libraries directories published between 1910 and 1957. He lists five major organizational groups maintaining special libraries: (1) business and industrial companies, (2) nonprofit associations and institution, (3) government agencies, (4) institutions of higher learning, and (5) large public library systems. By 1957 the largest number (47.6 percent) of special libraries were company libraries. The origins of the company libraries, their collection interests, significant librarians, patterns of development and other aspects of special library development are historically surveyed. The antecedents of special library service to business and industry, such as the early mechanics and merchantile libraries, are also covered.   338

LAUBACH, Harriet. Library Service to Business, Labor and Industry: Its Development in Libraries at Princeton, Akron, and Pittsburgh. Master's thesis, Carnegie Institute, 1952. 117 pp., bibl.

This paper is primarily a consideration of current (1952) library procedures and services. The author presents a historical discussion of each library before analyzing its present status. The libraries covered are (1) Industrial Relations Section, Princeton University; (2) Business and Labor Service, Akron Public Library; (3) University of Pittsburgh; and (4) Business Branch of the Carnegie Library of Pittsburgh. 339

Correctional Institution Libraries.

JOHNSON, Ruth Elaine. Libraries in Correctional Institutions. Master's thesis, Western Reserve, 1959. 123 pp., bibl. Section II of this paper (pages 24-41) deals with the history of prison libraries in the United States. This history extends from 1802, when the Kentucky State Reformatory began library service, up to the middle of the 20th century. After a general introduction the author presents brief histories of the libraries at the following penal institutions: (1) U. S. Penitentiary at Atlanta, (2) Menard Division of the Illinois State Penitentiary, (3) Sing Sing Prison, and (4) San Quentin. 340

PETTY, Wanda Eileen. The History of the Ohio Penitentiary Library. Master's thesis, Western Reserve, 1949. 67 pp., bibl. In 1839, the Reverend Charles Fitch saw the need for books for inmates of the Ohio Penitentiary and pushed for the establishment of a library there. His work was carried on by the Rev. J. B. Finley, who canvassed prison contractors and others and ran ads in newspapers until he had increased the collection from 300 to several thousand volumes. By 1885 a school library and a Catholic library had been added to the main library. This study covers to 1949, at which time the library, with no official appropriations, had grown to 10,000 volumes. 341

Medical Libraries

DONLEY, Virginia. A Chronology of Medical Libraries in the United States with Some Bibliographic Notes Pertaining to the Early History. Master's thesis, Western Reserve, 1957. 83 pp., bibl. This is a chronological history of important medical libraries. Information given for each includes: (1) date of establishment; (2) any disputed dates; (3) latest available size of collection; (4) name of person or organization responsible for original establishment; and (5) bibliographic notes on sources of information. This work is indexed. 342

FREUND, Clare E. The Library of the College of Physicians of Philadelphia. Master's thesis, Drexel Institute of Technology, 1951. 58 pp., bibl.
This is a history of the library of the College of Physicians of Philadelphia from 1791 to 1951, with emphasis on the decade 1941-1951. From 1791 to 1853 the college had no real home and the book collection was small. In 1863 the College of Physicians moved to its first real home and in 1864 acquired the 2,500 volume Lewis collection. By 1950 the collection had grown to some 170,000 volumes and the College and its library were now housed in a new building financed by a $100,000 grant from Andrew Carnegie. The library serves all the major branches of medicine except veterinary science and dentistry, which are covered by the University of Pennsylvania. The library of the College of Physicians has long considered it an obligation to provide a historical record of medicine and thus its collection is rich in the older classics.   343

Museum and Historical Society Libraries.

DUNIWAY, David C. The Administration of Six Selected State Historical Society Libraries: A Historical Study. Master's thesis, University of California, 1939. 80 pp., bibl.
The author traces the development up to 1935 of the libraries of the following historical societies: Massachusetts Historical Society, New York Historical Society, Pennsylvania Historical Society, Wisconsin Historical Society, Minnesota Historical Society, and the Society of California Pioneers. His major emphasis is on administration, with some consideration of the development of collections. 344

HESKIN, Mary Katheryn. The Philadelphia Commercial Museum Library, 1896-1952. Master's thesis, Drexel Institute of Technology, 1952. 40 pp., bibl.
The author traces the evolution of the library from a small reference department for the Bureau of Foreign Trade to its position in 1952 as an internationally known free library. The library was handicapped from the beginning by a lack of funds, but still managed to acquire one of the world's best collections relating to trade and commerce. By 1952 the collection numbered some 65,000 volumes.   345

LIBBY, David Carleton. The Library of the Chicago Historical Society: A Study. Master's thesis, University of Chicago, 1948. 136 pp., bibl.
The urge to preserve and perpetuate the American tradition in the early 19th century has been demonstrated as one of the major causal factors in the development of the

American public library. Mr. Libby traces the development
of the Chicago Historical Society's library from its establishment in 1856 up to the 1940's. Mr. Libby points out
that the library was a public one, open to all qualified
users, and that the Society's collections formed a major
part of the Chicago library picture.   346

PRESSING, Kirk L. The Library of the Historical Society of
Delaware. Master's thesis, Drexel Institute of Technology, 1954. 51 pp., bibl.
Presents the history of the development of the Historical
Society of Delaware and its library from 1864 to 1953. It
is divided into three sections: (1) history of the society; (2) history of the library; and (3) development of publication activities of the society, now under the library's jurisdiction. 347

SIMS, Elizabeth E. The Allen Memorial Art Museum Library,
Oberlin, Ohio; A Study. Master's thesis, Western Reserve,
1952. 73 pp., bibl.
This study traces the development of the collection from
1917. At that time the collection, which was quite small,
was transferred to the Allen Art Museum. By 1952 the
collection had grown to over 15,000 volumes and had been
recognized as outstanding by leading authorities. The author devotes part of this paper to the library's history,
while another part is devoted to a survey of current (1952)
conditions in the library.   348

WALDRON, Rodney K. A History of the Library of the State
Historical Society of Colorado, 1879-1940. Master's thesis,
University of Denver, 1950. 167 pp., bibl.
Chronologically traces the main steps in the evolution of
the library of the State Historical Society of Colorado, and
analyzes the contributions of a few highly influential people--
especially Will C. Ferrill, long-time curator of the collection. The author concerns himself mainly with the library's collections and personnel. He finds that the library's growth was slow and very uneven, and that so little
interest was evinced by the public and the library's early
administration that the library almost ceased to exist. A
consistent shortage of funds and numerous factional dis-
putes further hampered the library's growth.   349

WALKER, Muriel Hughes. The Library of the Western Reserve Historical Society. Master's thesis, Kent State University, 1952. 121 pp., bibl.
The first half of this paper deals with the history of the
library of the Western Reserve Historical Society from its
inception in 1867 to 1950. The author analyzes the reasons
for the library's rapid growth, its efforts to secure adequate quarters, the historical evolution of its special collections, and presents short biographical sketches of

significant contributors. 350

WOLF, Naomi E. The Library of the Genealogical Society of
Pennsylvania, 1892-1952. Master's thesis, Drexel Institute of Technology, 1953. 39 pp., bibl.
Traces the history of the Genealogical Society of Pennsylvania, and then describes the history of the library 1892-
1952. One chapter is devoted to the influence of three
members of the Leech family on the development of the
library. 351

Governmental Libraries

BREISACHER, Renata. A History and Survey of the Library of
the National Bureau of Standards. Master's thesis, Catholic University, 1953. 51 pp., bibl.
The first 20 pages of the paper trace the history of the
National Bureau of Standards Library from its beginning
in 1900 to 1953. The library was organized in answer to
the Bureau's needs for a collection to support its research.
By 1903 it contained some 1,000 volumes and by 1910 it
reached nearly 6,000 volumes. The author describes the
development of the library's organization, function, financial support and physical plant. 352

BRINKLEY, Clara. Army Post Library Service: An Inquiry into Its Origin and Development, Present Organization, and
Future. Master's thesis, University of Washington, 1952.
67 pp., bibl.
This first half of this paper deals with the development
of the Army Post Library Service from the Civil War,
when the first organized efforts were made, to the end of
the Second World War. At times the Army Post Library
System has stood as the largest public library system in
the world. During World War I over 6,000,000 books were
brought together for distribution to American soldiers. At
the same time some 36 post libraries were constructed
with funds from a Carnegie grant. The Army Library Service has traditionally been curtailed during peace time and
plunged into feverish activity at time of war. 353

GOLDMAN, Sylvia. History of the United States Weather Bureau Library. Master's thesis, Catholic University, 1959.
95 pp., bibl.
In 85 years the Weather Bureau Library grew from a
small reference collection in the study room of the Chief
Signal Offices of the War Department in Washington, to a
large collection of over 100,000 volumes, maps, photo-
graphs, motion pictures, and slides. This thesis describes
that development from 1870 to 1960. It is divided into
three major sections: (1) the history of the Weather Bureau;

(2) history of the Weather Bureau Library; and (3) present-day functions of the Library at its new location in Suitland, Maryland.   354

HENCH, Marcia. The Library of the Supreme Court of the United States. Master's thesis, Drexel Institute of Technology, 1951. 43 pp., bibl.
This study begins with a brief history of the Court, stressing only the important points from its establishment in 1789. The period from 1789 to 1801 is not covered since during this time the Court used the library facilities of Philadelphia and New York, and no individual court library was established. Until 1807 the Clerk of the Court acted as librarian, but in that year the first librarian, Henry D. Clarke, was appointed. The author emphasizes the history of the library from 1887 to 1932.   355

HUDON, Edward Gerard. The Library Facilities of the Supreme Court of the United States: A Historical Study. Master's thesis, Catholic University, 1956. 88 pp., bibl.
This study traces the evolution of the Library of the Supreme Court from 1790 to 1955. For several years after 1790 there was no library for the Supreme Court, and it was not until Marshall became Chief Justice that the library made its feeble start. Since then its growth has been slow but steady, culminating in some 180,000 volumes in two libraries. Mr. Hudon emphasizes the development and characteristics of the library collections.   356

NORTH, Norma. O. A. E. S. L. A History of the Library of the Ohio Agricultural Experiement Station at Wooster, Ohio. Master's thesis, Western Reserve, 1953. 60 pp., bibl.
First established in 1882, this library developed very slowly and did not merit a librarian until 1911. William K. Greenbank was the first official librarian, and the author describes his administration (1911-1922) in detail. The period from 1923 to 1947 saw a succession of four women librarians, who were unable to stop a deterioration of the library over the 20-year period. The greatest difficulty appeared in their inability to classify and catalog the collection. Several reasons for the problem were lack of trained personnel and inadequate financial support. The author explains that this was probably due to the fact that the station was not associated with a college or university, as were many of the better station libraries. The author concludes with a discussion of the development of departmental libraries at the station.   357

SCOTT, Catherine Dorothy. The History and Present Status of the Library of the United States Tariff Commission. Master's thesis, Catholic University, 1955. 81 pp., bibl. Published: ACRL Microcard #53.

Traces the history of the Tariff Commission Library
from its inception in 1917, in the newly created Commission, up to 1955. Originally for the use of the Commission's experts, the Tariff Library has tended to serve an
ever-widening clientele. Since 1921 it has done extensive
inter-library loan work and now serves the public as well
as government employees. The author finds that the Tariff
Library was amply supported from its inception and that
its growth has been steady.   358
THOMAS, Mary Anne. The Delaware State Archives: 1931-1951.
    Master's thesis, Drexel Institute of Technology, 1952. 53
    pp., bibl.
    Presents an account of the development and activities of
    the Delaware State Archives 1931-1951. A brief introduc-
    tion describes archival methods in Delaware before 1905,
    and the founding and early work of the Public Archives
    Commission.   359
WILLIS, Dawn Eliza. The History and Present Status of the
    Library of the United States Geological Survey. Master's
    thesis, Catholic University, 1953. 62 pp., bibl.
    Traces the history of the Geological Survey Library from
    1882, when it was established, to 1953. By 1953 the Li-
    brary had grown from a small collection of 1,000 volumes
    to one of the world's best geological libraries, containing
    over 250,000 volumes and 100,000 maps. Special emphasis
    is placed on the development of staff, collections, and
    quarters. A short history of the U.S. Geological Survey
    is included.   360

Other Special Libraries.

BROMILEY, Francis. The History and Organization of the
    Franklin D. Roosevelt Library, Hyde Park, New York.
    Master's thesis, Western Reserve, 1959. 108 pp., bibl.
    Published: ACRL Microcard #117.
    Traces the history of the Roosevelt Library from 1939,
    when the bill to accept the Library for maintenance by
    the U.S. Government was defeated in the House of Rep-
    resentatives by a vote of 139 to 229, up to 1959. Empha-
    sizes services, collections and physical plant.   361
BROWN, Ruth Ellen. History of Special Libraries in Denver,
    Colorado, 1861-1953. Master's thesis, University of Chi-
    cago, 1955. 225 pp., bibl.
    The author traces the history of the development of special
    libraries in Denver from their rather slow beginning with
    only nine established by 1900, to 1953 when the city had
    62 full-fledged special libraries. The author covers almost
    every phase of library service in Denver, including public

library service under the leadership of such great librarians as John Cotton Dana and Chalmers Hadley. She also treats college and university special libraries (i.e., departmental). Appendix I. is a chronological list of special libraries established in Denver 1861-1953.   362

COWLES, Lois Hart. The First Century of the Library of the New Britain Institute. Master's thesis, Western Reserve, 1951. 92 pp., bibl.
After first surveying the history of libraries in New Britain, Connecticut, up to 1850, the author traces the history of the New Britain Institute Library from 1853 to 1953. The author treats the development of the Institute's library in detail, outlining its difficulties and achievements. In 1901 a new building was erected, at which time the city agreed to finance the library with $4,000 annually. The period 1901-1921 saw the collection grow rapidly; however the rate of growth decreased with the advent of the depression and another war. Nevertheless, in 1950 the collection numbered over 90,000 volumes.   363

GLADECK, Alberta Alma. The Library of the Franklin Institute. Master's thesis, Drexel Institute of Technology, 1953. 35 pp., bibl. Published: ACRL Microcard #37.
Traces the history of the library of the Franklin Institute (founded 1820) from a small collection kept in the homes of the library committee to a scientific library of over 200,000 volumes housed in a wing of the Franklin Institute in Philadelphia. The Journal of the Franklin Institute and the library's cataloging and classification system are given special attention.   364

KAHN, Rose Ann. A History of the Peabody Institute Library, Baltimore, Maryland, 1857-1916. Master's thesis, Catholic University, 1953. 87 pp., bibl. Published: ACRL Microcard #16.
After a brief survey of library development in Baltimore prior to the Civil War and a short account of the life of George Peabody, the author traces the history of the Peabody Institute Library from its inception in 1857 up to 1916. The author finds that throughout the library's history the public had been critical of its services. She points out that Peabody planned the library as a reference collection and never intended that it be a popular library, and that the administration of the Peabody Institute Library complied with his wishes.   365

LEASURE, Marilyn F. A History of the Libraries of the Baltimore and Ohio Railroad Company. Master's thesis, Drexel Institute of Technology, 1954. 31 pp., bibl.
This paper is divided into five parts: (1) a brief history of the Baltimore and Ohio Railroad; (2) the history of the

129

railroad's early circulating library (1885-1931); (3) the
early development of the research library now called the
Employee's Library (1944-1951); (4) the library 1951-1954;
and (5) conclusion. The author found that the library established in 1885 was dependent upon the well-being of the
B & O Railroad. In the depression of 1931 the library was
closed. In 1944 a central library was opened to provide
services to anyone desiring information on the B & O, its
history, organization and development. By 1950 the collection had grown to over 12,000 volumes.   366

SMAIL. H. Arlene. A History of the Eleanor Squire Memorial
Library of the Garden Center of Greater Cleveland. Master's thesis, Western Reserve, 1955. 63 pp., bibl.
This history of a unique special library spans a period of
25 years, 1930-1955. It originally served only as a reference and research collection, but in 1937 a small lending collection was established. Librarian Marjorie B. Clel-
land guided the collection from 1938 to 1940, and prepared
a Classification Scheme for a Garden Center Library of
Books, which was published in 1940. The collection today
numbers 7,000 volumes, many of them rare, and serves
a valuable research function in Cleveland.   367

VARNER, Sister Christina. The Development of Special Libraries in St. Paul and Minneapolis, Minnesota, 1849-1949.
Master's thesis, University of Chicago, 1950. 152 pp.,
bibl.
This study gives a history of all types of library service
in St. Paul-Minneapolis for the period covered. University, college, and public library development are treated,
as well as special libraries. However, the emphasis is on
special library development in St. Paul-Minneapolis in the
20th century. A chronological list of special libraries
1849-1949 is included.   368

School Libraries

General Studies.

HAMMITT, Frances Eleanor. School Library Legislation in
Indiana, Illinois, and Wisconsin: A Historical Study. Doctoral dissertation, University of Chicago, 1948. 266 pp.,
bibl.
Begins by tracing the history of school libraries, especially in the Mid-West, and then devotes three chapters to a
discussion of school library legislation in each state up
to 1940. The final chapter is a synthesis of the data. The
author finds many similarities in the approach to school
library legislation taken by the three states; however,

Wisconsin got a somewhat slower start than did the other
two. An Appendix includes a chronological list of library
laws for the three states up to 1940.   369

RUFSVOLD, Margaret I. Library Service to Schools in the
    South since 1900. Master's thesis, George Peabody Col-
    lege for Teachers, 1933. Published: Peabody Contributions
    to Librarianship #1. 1934.
    Traces the history of school libraries in the South from
    1900 to 1933. The author finds that school library develop-
    ment was slow and haphazard up to 1925, but that re-
    markable growth was effected from 1925 to 1933. Two fac-
    tors were central to this growth: (1) the adoption of re-
    vised high school library standards in 1929; and (2) the
    interest of the Julius Rosenwald Fund in school and coun-
    ty library development. Despite the rapid growth, the
    school libraries of the South were still only in the begin-
    ning stages of development in 1933. The author lists a
    number of factors responsible for this slow development. 370

Local Studies Arranged by State.

Connecticut

BELL, Dorothy. History of School Libraries in Connecticut,
    1839-1860. Master's thesis, Southern Connecticut State
    College, 1964. 123 pp., bibl.
    The author begins with a description of Henry Barnard's
    efforts to establish school libraries in Connecticut from
    1839 to 1842. She then turns to an analysis of the work
    of two other superintendents, John D. Philbrick, 1855-
    1857 and David N. Camp, 1857-1860. In 1839 Barnard
    noted only six school libraries in Connecticut's 1400
    schools. By 1860 there were nearly 600, with collections
    totaling over 40,000 volumes. Catalogs of several of the
    collections are included in the Appendix.   371

Georgia

SONGER, Florence Hooten. Development of Public School Li-
    braries in Georgia, 1890-1950. Master's thesis, University
    of North Carolina, 1955. 143 pp., bibl.
    Traces the history of public school library development in
    Georgia, from the first efforts of the Georgia Teacher's
    Association in 1894 to initiate a reading circle in the pub-
    lic schools up to 1950. The growth of school library ser-
    vice in Georgia was slow until 1940. From 1940 to 1950
    growth was greatly accelerated due to state financial sup-
    port and supervisory direction.   372

Illinois

NOONAN, Mabel Z. The Development of Libraries in the Chicago Public Elementary Schools. Master's thesis, De Paul University, 1953. 99 pp., bibl.
The first 50 pages of this paper trace the development of libraries of the Chicago Elementary Schools from 1899 to 1952. In that time the average appropriation for library expenditures per school rose from $33.33 to $1,095.21. The author finds that from 1883 to 1952 the Chicago Public Library was instrumental in providing loan collections for the elementary schools, and it still plays a vital role, although not to such a great extent. The WPA project in Chicago Elementary Schools gave great impetus to library development from 1935 to 1941. It was during this time that the first elementary school librarian was appointed, and by 1952 the number of elementary school librarians had grown to 317. The author also traces the development of training for Chicago elementary school librarians and the development of the collections. 373

Indiana

CARROLL, Floy Caroline. School Library Development in Indiana. Master's thesis, University of Illinois, 1929. 69 pp., bibl.
Gives the history of the growth and decline of township school libraries in Indiana and analyzes the causes of their successes and failures. The period covered is from the establishment of township school libraries in 1852 to 1899, when legislation was passed that led to the demise of the earlier township library system. A brief survey of library development in the state from 1806 to 1852 is included. Public indifference and a consistent lack of funds are considered the basic causes for the failure of the township libraries. 374

Kentucky

GALLOWAY, M. Louise. The Historical Development and Present Status of Public High School Libraries in Kentucky; 1908 to 1950. Master's thesis, Columbia, 1951. 163 pp., bibl.
This is an analysis of white and Negro public high school libraries in Kentucky from the inception of a statewide system of high schools in 1908 to 1950. The author says that information relating to high school libraries in Kentucky was fragmentary and difficult to locate, but it seems

that the first full-time high school librarians were employed in Louisville in 1916. Library development received considerable impetus from the adoption in 1923 of
state regulations for school libraries. Development of
high school library services in Kentucky remained slow
and torturous to 1950, with the most serious retardation
occurring during World War II.   375

Maryland

WILLIAMS, Sister Mary Leona. History and Description of the
  Baltimore Archdiocesan Library Council. Master's thesis,
  Catholic University, 1960. 102 pp. , bibl.
  Traces the history of the Baltimore Archdiocesan Library
  Council from its establishment in 1946 to 1958. Illustrates
  the BALC's efforts to present a library program for all
  the Catholic schools in the Diocese. The efforts included
  sponsoring annual Catholic Book Week programs, publishing book lists, and pushing for a central library in each
  school. The author finds they were highly successful in
  the latter activity.   376

Minnesota

BRIGGS, Margaret Irene. The Development of Public School
  Libraries in Minnesota, 1861-1938. Master's thesis, University of Chicago, 1945. 136 pp. , bibl.
  Few books or other educational materials were available
  to Minnesota school children in the 19th century. The
  first state appropriation was made in 1887, $10,000 for
  the school libraries of the whole state. At the same time
  a public school library commission was established, and
  by 1900 over 300,000 volumes had been purchased. The
  author traces the history of these collections and points
  out the importance of the work of two librarians, Miss
  Clara Baldwin and Miss Martha Wilson, who prepared
  book lists, inspected libraries, and gave instruction to
  would-be school librarians until courses for credit were
  provided at the University of Minnesota in 1923. Major
  library developments in the state occurred after 1915. An
  appendix includes a list of books circulated 10 or more
  times in Minnesota schools 1899-1900.   377

New Jersey

LANE, Margaret. The Development of Library Service to Public Schools in New Jersey. Master's thesis, Columbia University, 1938. 177 pp. , bibl.

This study covers the development of school libraries in
New Jersey from the mid-1800's to 1937. Development
was very slow until 1913, with few good collections being
established. The 25-year period from 1913 to 1937 saw
some 245 high school libraries established in New Jersey,
but elementary school library development was less marked. Such matters as the training and certification of school
librarians, state aid, and the development of county library service are also examined.   378

New York

TINKLEPAUGH, Doris Kellogg. School Libraries in New York
State; Their History from 1890 to 1930. Master's thesis,
Columbia University, 1937. 113 pp., bibl.
Traces the history of school library development in New
York State, showing the general growth of school libraries from the days when no restrictions or qualifications
were imposed to the time when standards for school library service were defined and enforced throughout the
state. Discusses the aid and encouragement that state government gave to school library development, and analyzes
the role of the school library in the state of New York
from 1890 to 1930.   379

North Carolina

REDDING, Bobbie Newman. The Developmental History of the
Elementary School Libraries in Guilford County, North
Carolina. Master's thesis, University of North Carolina,
1957. 71 pp., bibl.
The author traces the development of the elementary school
libraries in three Guilford County school systems--Greens-
boro, Guilford County, and High Point--through the use of
statistics from the State School Library Advisor's Office
in Raleigh. These statistics were studied at five-year in-
tervals from 1935-1936 to 1955-1956. Special areas covered are enrollment, librarians, expenditures, collections,
circulation, and quarters. The author also examines the
effects of centralized authority in each of the systems. 380

Ohio

ALDRICH, Frederic De Long. History of Ohio Public School
Library Legislation. Doctoral dissertation, Western Reserve, 1953. 209 pp., bibl. Published: Scarecrow Press,
1959.
This study deals with Ohio legislation for elementary and

secondary school libraries from 1785 to 1953. In 1853
Ohio reorganized its school system and set up a statewide school district system. It met considerable opposition because of the increased tax burden, the small collections, and the difficulties encountered in servicing
rural areas. These difficulties led to the complete abandon-
ment of the libraries in 1868. School libraries did not
gain real strength again until after 1902. From then on libraries have developed steadily in Ohio. 381

Pennsylvania

MELVIN, Sister M. C. History of Public School Libraries in
Pennsylvania. Doctoral dissertation, University of Chicago, 1962. 600 pp., bibl. Not examined. 382

South Carolina

WOFFORD, Azile. The History and Present Status of School
Libraries in South Carolina, 1868-1938. Master's thesis,
Columbia University, 1938. 134 pp., bibl.
The first 60 pages of this paper cover the history of
school libraries in South Carolina, beginning with the establishment of public schools in 1868 and ending with 1938.
Only brief attention is given to libraries in South Carolina
before the Civil War, and no coverage is given to libraries in Negro schools. The author presents reasons why
school libraries developed more slowly in South Carolina
than in any of the other Southern states, the most notable
reason being the lack of state aid. 383

Texas

DONALDSON, La Nelle Love. A Decade and a Half with the
School Libraries of Texas. Master's thesis, Texas State
College, 1954. 84 pp., bibl.
School libraries in Texas were slow to develop. The greatest growth has occurred since 1940, despite the interrup-
tions caused by World War II, so the author has chosen
to treat here the period from 1940 to 1954. This study
surveys the events that contributed to school library development in the state, such as standards and legislation,
with little coverage of individual libraries or librarians. 384
FEENEY, Renee Bougoyne. The History and Development of
the Library in the Public Schools of Houston, Texas. Master's thesis, Texas State College, 1954. 82 pp., bibl.
This paper traces the development of school libraries in
Houston from the first establishment of a small classroom

collection in 1882 up through 1953. In the beginning students were encouraged to bring their own reading matter from home, but this soon proved unworkable. Later the Houston Public Library stepped in to fill the gap and served as a school materials center for many years. The first full-time school librarian was appointed in 1924. The author finds the period after 1949 the most significant in terms of development, for during that time the number of elementary school libraries tripled and the secondary school collections were strengthened.   385

HOLDEN, Opal. The History of Library Service in Austin Public Schools. Master's thesis, University of Texas, 1962. 72 pp., bibl.
This study traces the library services offered in the Austin, Texas, public schools from 1886 to 1962. The first school library in Austin was located in the Austin High School. It had its beginnings in a resolution passed by the School Board in 1886 appropriating 25 dollars for the purchase of "classical literature of American and English Authors." From 1900 on the Austin public schools grew rapidly and library development paralleled that growth. In 1960 every one of the 60 schools in the Austin public school system had a library with a trained librarian in charge. These libraries contained some 200,000 books, about 6-1/2 books for each child in the system.   386

MOORE, Mattie Ruth. Southern Association, State and Local Leadership for Library Service in Texas Schools. Master's thesis, University of Texas, 1955. 101 pp., bibl.
The historical portion of this paper describes the kind of leadership that has appeared for the improvement of library service in Texas schools. The author also examines the history of regional and state leadership for school library service, and she traces the transfer of major responsibility from the region to the state and local school districts. The time span covered is 1895-1953.   387

Virginia

DUNKLEY, Grace Croom. Development of Public School Libraries in Virginia with Emphasis on the Period 1958-1959 Through 1963-1964. Master's thesis, University of North Carolina, 1965. 82 pp., bibl.
The author reviews the first 50 years of school library history in Virginia, supplying a detailed quantitative analysis of school library development for the years 1958-1959 through 1963-1964. School library progress in Virginia was mainly due to the financial aid provided by the state. That aid, which began with the sum of $5,000 in 1908,

had grown to over $600,000 in 1958. School library growth was also stimulated by the appointment of a State School Library Supervisor in 1923. The author finds that there has been a distinct trend toward the establishment of central libraries in elementary schools, but that the majority of school libraries in Virginia are still located in the high schools.   388

HOYLE, Nancy Elizabeth. A Study of the Development of Library Service in the Public Schools of Virginia. Master's thesis, Columbia University, 1938. 168 pp., bibl.
This study traces the development of library service for the public schools of Virginia from 1870 to 1938. The author points out how social, economic, and educational conditions, and the lack of public library provision, influenced the development of school libraries in Virginia. There was little interest in establishing school libraries in Virginia until a law was passed in 1906 setting up public high schools. Development was slow up to 1931, but increased rapidly from then until 1938. The author discusses the development of standards, education for school librarians, state aid to public school libraries and other influential factors.   389

Washington

FOSTER, Patricia M. Historical and Descriptive Study of the Bellevue Public School Library System and of its Administrative Pattern with Implications for the Future. Master's thesis, University of Washington, 1960. Not examined.   390

Wisconsin

SKAAR, Martha O. Public School Libraries in Wisconsin: A Historical Study of School Libraries Under the Supervision of the State Department of Public Instruction. Master's thesis, Columbia University, 1938. 93 pp., bibl.
The author traces the history of school libraries in Wisconsin from 1848, when the first feeble efforts were made, until 1937, when they were relatively well-established. The first 40 years (1848-1887) of the school library movement in Wisconsin formed a period of struggle and uncertainty, while the 50-year period from 1887 to 1937 was one of slow but steady progress.   391

State Libraries

Local Studies Arranged by State.

VanMALE, John Edward. A History of Library Extension in
Colorado, 1890-1930. Master's thesis, University of Denver, 1940. 100 pp., bibl.
The author begins his study with a brief survey of the
"library extension idea" in America. He then traces the
development of library extension services in Colorado,
which began with John Cotton Dana's efforts in 1890 to
serve rural patrons of the Denver Public Library. The
first serious efforts at statewide extension services took
place after 1900, with a Clubwomen's Commission handling
the administration of the traveling libraries. In 1930 the
Clubwomen's Commission and the Colorado Library Commission were consolidated and given a budget of $9,000.
The author describes the pioneering efforts of Chalmers
Hadley and Malcolm Wyer, both librarians at the Denver
Public Library.   392

Connecticut

HANDY, Catherine Hickey. The Connecticut State Library,
1851-1936. Master's thesis, Southern Connecticut, 1965.
115 pp., bibl.
The author begins her paper with a history of American
state libraries from their first beginnings in the 18th century up through the 20th. The author then considers the
reasons for the founding of the Connecticut State Library.
She feels that it evolved from state needs concerning the
care of the book collection, the keeping of records, and
the management of systems of exchange. A library committee was set up in 1851 and the first Connecticut State
Librarian was appointed in 1854. The story of the library's
development from that time until 1936 is divided into sections corresponding to the terms of its librarians: (1) I.
Hammond Trumbull, 1854-1855; (2) Charles J. Hoadly,
1855-1900; and (3) George S. Goddard, 1900-1936. Appendix A includes "Selected Legislation Relating to the Connecticut State Library."   393

Florida

CHALKER, William Jennings. The Historical Development of
the Florida State Library, 1845-1959. Master's thesis,
George Peabody College for Teachers, 1951. 70 pp., bibl.
Begins with a brief consideration of the state library in
the United States and then presents a history of the Florida State Library up to 1949. The Florida State Library,

like so many before it, began with miscellaneous collections of books accumulated in the offices of various state officials. In 1855 the Secretary of State was made the official state librarian and $100 was appropriated for binding and shelving the books. In 1925 an act was passed establishing the present Florida State Library. In 1927 W. T. Cash was appointed State Librarian and inherited a collection of 2,500 volumes. Growth was rapid under his directorship despite a serious shortage of funds. 394

Louisiana

STEPHENSON, Harriet Shirley. History of the Louisiana State Library, Formerly Louisiana Library Commission. Doctoral dissertation, Louisiana State University, 1957. 492 pp., bibl. (D. A. 58-4705)
This study traces the impact of the Louisiana State Library, from its inception in 1920 as the Louisiana Library Commission through 1955, on public library development in the state. Dr. Stephenson has divided her work into seven major chronological sections. The first section surveys the condition of public libraries in Louisiana in the early 20th century. The rest of this paper reveals the highly influential role the State Library played in public library development in the state. Passage of a modern public library law, the use of demonstration libraries to raise public support, working toward the establishment of a library school at Louisiana State University, the establishment of a statewide reference service for Negroes, and an ever active public relations program were some of the more significant achievements of the State Library. This work also throws light on the career of Essae M. Culver, Executive Secretary of the Library Commission and one-time president of the American Library Association. 395

Maryland

COOVER, Robert Wingert. A History of the Maryland State Library, 1827-1939. Master's thesis, Catholic University, 1956. 179 pp., bibl. Published: ACRL Microcard #88.
Traces the history of the Maryland State Library from 1827, when it was established, through 1939. The collection grew very slowly; its holdings in 1909 numbered only 40,000 volumes. By 1939 the collection had increased to over 110,000 volumes, primarily law books to serve the Maryland State Legislature. The paper discusses the staff, collections, physical plant and services of the library for

the period covered. 396

New Mexico

BARRETT, Mildred A. Development of Library Extension in
New Mexico. Master's thesis, Western Reserve, 1958. 143
pp., bibl. Published: ACRL, Microcard #97.
Briefly sketches library development and attempts at library extension up to 1929, then traces the history of the
New Mexico Library Extension Service, and its contributions to the New Mexico library scene, from its inception
in 1929 up to 1958. The service, with no quarters of its
own, no book fund, and no books, was a "child of charity" during its early years. However, qualified professional
leadership and wide support insured its success. The author traces the efforts of the service to fulfill its major
purpose--promotion of library development in New Mexico. 397

New York

VLOEBERGH, Helen Elizabeth. A History of the New York
State Library from 1818 to 1905. Master's thesis, Catholic University, 1956. 76 pp., bibl. Published: ACRL Microcard #83.
This paper traces the history of the New York State Library from its inception in 1818 until 1905, when Melvil
Dewey resigned as Director. The library was originally
founded as a reference collection for state officials, but
when Dewey became Director in 1888 he extended its services to all the people of New York. The author points
out, however, that the State Library always remained essentially a reference library and never functioned as a
true public library. The State Library's considerable influence on library development in New York is related,
with special reference to school and public library development. 398

Tennessee

SETTLEMIRE, Claude L. The Tennessee State Library, 1854-
1923. Master's thesis, George Peabody College for Teachers, 1951. 38 pp., bibl.
This paper presents a history of the Tennessee State Library from its establishment in 1854 until it became a
division of the State Department of Education in 1923.
When the library was established the Secretary of State
acted as librarian, and the first state librarian was not

appointed until 1856. The author emphasizes the legislative development of the State Library. 399

Texas

PEACE, William Kittrell, III. A History of the Texas State
Library with Emphasis on the Period from 1930 to 1958.
Master's thesis, University of Texas, 1959. 98 pp., bibl.
Studies the history of the Texas State Library from its
inception in 1851 through 1958, with emphasis on the last
28 years. Considers the history of the overall administration of the library, the services and administration of the
various divisions, and the administration of the program
for developing rural library service under the Library Services Act. 400

Types of Library Service

Cataloging and Classification.

BATES, N. P. History of the Classification and Cataloging
of Maps As Shown in Printed Catalogs of Sixteen U. S.
Libraries Issued from 1827-1907. Master's thesis, University of North Carolina, 1954. 74 pp., Not examined. 401
CORCORAN, Sara R. A Study of Cataloging Practice Through
1830 As Shown in Printed Book Catalogs of Six Libraries
of the City of New York. Master's thesis, Columbia University, 1936. 76 pp., bibl.
The author begins this study with a survey of library history in colonial New York, noting specially the work of
the Reverend Thomas Bray. Histories of the six libraries
covered in this study are then presented. They are the
New York Society Library, the New York Hospital Library,
the New York Historical Society Library, the Apprentices'
Library, the Mercantile Library and the Lyceum of Natural History Library. The catalogs of these libraries are
examined in hopes of discovering trends toward a modern
cataloging practice. However there was little indication of
any development during the period covered (1758-1831),
and the author found only one attempt at the establishment
of rules for the preparation of a catalog. Comparisons of
entries from the early catalogs with modern practice point
out the inadequacy and lack of uniformity of the early
catalogs. 402
GORE, Daniel Jack, Jr. The Schomberg Collection and Its
Catalog: A Historical Sketch. Master's thesis, University
of North Carolina, 1963. 63 pp., bibl.

The author has aimed at illustrating historically the ways
in which a library catalog will be affected by the changing
character and objectives of the collection it records. He
has chosen the Schomberg Collection of Negro Literature
and History, a branch of the New York Public Library,
for his subject. The first part of his paper is devoted to
a history of the collection's development from 1925 to
1960, while the second part deals with the catalog. Gore
concludes that catalogs of special collections should not
be built to a standard, but should be constructed with
close regard to the collections they describe.   403

GRAZIANO, Eugene Edward. The Philosophy of Hegel as
Basis for the Dewey Decimal Classification Schedule. Master's thesis, University of Oklahoma, 1955. 70 pp. , bibl.
This paper begins with a survey of classification in the
United States from 1850 to 1876. The author then discusses the pioneering classification scheme devised by William Torrey Harris at the St. Louis Public Library in
1870. The author documents his belief that Torrey's classification system was based largely on Hegel's philosophy.
He also argues that Dewey adapted his subject divisions
from the Harris Scheme, and thus the Dewey Decimal
Classification traces its lineage back to Hegel's philosophy,
not to Bacon's as is sometimes maintained.   404

HEISS, Ruth Miriam. The Card Catalog in Libraries of the
United States Before 1876. Master's thesis, University of
Illinois, 1938. 91 pp. , bibl.
The tremendous growth of American libraries in the 19th
century forced librarians to find new methods of preparing catalogs. Taking note of the use of card catalogs in
foreign countries, especially France, they turned to this
form. After 1853, due to Jewett's pressure for a national
catalog using cards and the publicity given card catalogs
at the Librarian's Conference of 1853, the card catalog
spread across the country. The Philadelphia Library Company pioneered in card catalogs for public use in 1857,
and Ezra Abbot and C. A. Cutter produced a model catalog at Harvard in 1861. The author discusses the problems involved in the evolution of the card catalog, such
as the size and weight of cards, the most desirable form,
and the best method of storage. Foreign influences and
the leadership of such Americans as Charles Folsom,
Ezra Abbot, Charles Coffin Jewett, and Charles Ammi Cutter are treated.   405

HENSEL, Evelyn Mildred. History of the Catalog Department
of the University of Illinois Library. Master's thesis, University of Illinois, 1936. 100 pp. , bibl.

Traces the history of the Department from 1868 to 1932
in four chapters. Chapter one discusses cataloging at the
library before 1897, when the first professional librarian
was hired. Prior to this time cataloging was done by student assistants. In 1894 the Decimal classification was
adopted. Chapter two covers the Department from 1897
to 1906, when Katherine Sharp was librarian and Margaret
Mann was head (1897-1899) of the Catalog Department.
Chapter three treats the period from 1906 to 1932, most
of which time Phineas Windsor was Director of the Library. The Department grew rapidly from three catalogers
in 1906 to 18 in 1932. The fourth chapter covers the history of the Union Catalog at the University of Illinois Li-
brary.   406

OSBORN, Velva Jeanne. A History of Cooperative Cataloging
in the United States. Master's thesis, University of Chicago, 1944. 144 pp., bibl.
Beginning with first attempts in 1850, the author traces
the history of cooperative cataloging up to the middle of
the 20th century. The first such effort was made in 1850
by Charles Coffin Jewett in his suggestion for making the
Smithsonian Institution a national center. His idea failed,
and it was not until Cutter, Dewey, Poole, Fletcher and
others founded the American Library Association in 1876
that any more work was done in that direction. The important contribution of the Library of Congress is considered,
but the author concludes that much still needs to be
done.   407

OSWALD, Janet F. The Development of the Medical Subject
Heading. Master's thesis, Drexel Institute of Technology,
1955, 65 pp., bibl.
Traces the development of medical subject headings from
Dewey in 1876 to 1955, with reference to their use in
medical libraries in the United States. The leadership
of the Armed Forces Medical Library, and the continu-
ance of its work as the National Medical Library, are
emphasized.   408

PALMER, Vivian D. A Brief History of Cataloging Codes in
the United States, 1852-1949. Master's thesis, University
of Chicago, 1963. 100 pp., bibl.
The author briefly traces the history of the following
codes: (1) Pannizzi's; (2) Jewett's; (3)Cutter's; (4) Dewey's;
(5) the Anglo-American Code; and (6) Library of Congress
Code.   409

RANZ, James. The History of the Printed Book Catalogue in
the United States. Doctoral dissertation, University of
Illinois, 1960. 327 pp., bibl. Published: American Library
Association, 1964.

This study, emphasizing the period from the early 18th century to the late 19th century, is concerned with the rise and fall of the book catalog in America. Dr. Ranz provides an introductory survey of the history of catalogs from ancient times to 1700. He covers the development of the first book catalogs in colonial America, the sophistication of catalogs in later periods, and throws light on the contributions and conflicts of men like Poole, Abbot and Jewett. He concludes by discussing the demise of the book catalog in the last quarter of the 19th century. Three factors are cited as major in this demise: (1) the rapid growth of library collections; (2) the increased role of the catalog in a service-minded library era; and (3) the development of the L. C. card distribution system. Primary sources for the study were over 2,000 printed library catalogs.   410

RUFFIN, Mary Beverley. Some Developments Toward Modern Cataloging Practice in University Libraries as Exemplified in the Printed Book Catalogs of Harvard and Yale Before 1876. Master's thesis, Columbia University, 1935. 68 pp., bibl.
The author examines the printed book catalogs of the college library collection of each university, and also of the various societies and professional schools of Harvard and Yale before 1876. The author found many pioneering steps toward better cataloging before 1876, but they lacked uniformity and were highly localized. Individuality in cataloging was quite prevalent before the day of formal cataloging codes.   411

SERVIES, James Albert. Thomas Jefferson and His Bibliographic Classification. Master's thesis, University of Chicago, 1950. 119 pp., bibl.
This paper is divided into three major portions. Part one considers several of the major schemes developed during the early period in American history. Part two (Chapters II, III, IV and V), the largest section, deals with Jefferson's pragmatic scheme for the classification of knowledge. Mr. Servies considers its use at the Library of Congress and the University of Virginia and traces the changes the system underwent at Jefferson's and other classifiers' hands up to 1826. The final portion deals with a synthesis of Jefferson's thinking on the classification of knowledge.   412

STRAKA, Mildred. A Historical Review of the Cataloging Department of the Columbia University Libraries; 1883-1950. Master's thesis, Columbia University, 1951. 104 pp., bibl.
Traces the historical development of the Cataloging Department at Columbia from 1883 to 1950. The subject is

treated topically under the following chapter headings: (1)
Organization; (2) Staff; (3) Working conditions; (4) Physical
conditions; (5) The catalogs; (6) Procedures and routines
in the cataloging department; and (7) Policies and trends.
The author finds that the cataloging department at Columbia has shown a willingness to pursue change ever since
Melvil Dewey's tenure as Director.   413

THACKSTON, Frances Venable. The Development of Cataloging in the Libraries of Duke University and the University of North Carolina from Their Establishment to 1953.
Master's thesis, University of North Carolina, 1959. 107
pp., bibl. Published: ACRL Microcard #124.
After presenting a brief history of the two universities
and their libraries from 1795 to 1953, the author traces
the development of cataloging in the two libraries from
the late 18th century up to 1953. This narrative shows
the transition in the two libraries from manuscript book
catalog to the card catalog and from fixed-location sym-
bols to expandable call numbers. Over two million volumes
were available in the two libraries in 1953.   414

WILKINS, Madeleine J. History and Evaluation of Subject
Heading Approach in Medicine; A Study of Certain Medical Indexes Published in the United States. Master's thesis, Catholic University, 1955. 87 pp., bibl.
The author traces the history of the following medical
bibliographies: (1) Armed Forces Medical Library Catalog;
(2) Current List of Medical Literature; and (3) Quarterly
Cumulative Index Medicus.   415

WILLET, Mary McLeod. A History and Survey of the Nassau
County Library Association Union Catalog. Master's thesis, Drexel Institute of Technology, 1955. 46 pp., bibl.
This paper presents a history of the Nassau County Library Association Union Catalog from its inception to
1955 and briefly surveys the catalog's methods of providing service in 1955. The author finds that the union catalog, usually considered a research tool for large libraries,
proved an excellent way for small Nassau County libraries to provide better service to their patrons through
mutual cooperation. The cooperative association had nearly 30 members in 1954.   416

Reference.

ADAMS, E. M., Jr. A Study of Reference Librarianship in
the American College: 1876-1955. Master's thesis, East
Texas State, 1956. 61 pp., bibl.
Three events that occurred in 1876 stimulated the development of reference service in college libraries: the

establishment of the American Library Association; the establishment of the Library Journal, with its many aids to reference work; and Samuel S. Green's address to the American Library Association, in which he advocated the radical idea that librarians should help patrons select books and locate information. College librarians were quick to grasp this principle. Green's influence, plus the increase in graduate instruction and the discarding of the single textbook method, pressured libraries into offering reference service. This service, at first part-time and casual, grew to involve a full-time reference librarian working with all types of materials and finally developed to the specialization of various members within the department. The author finds that organized reference service was slow to develop in many colleges (Harvard 1939, Cornell 1947), basically for financial reasons.   417

McBRIDE, Margarete. Reference Service for Congress Before 1915. Master's thesis, Drexel Institute of Technology, 1955. 76 pp., bibl.
This study investigates the nature and extent of reference services to Congress by the Library of Congress before the Legislative Reference Service was established in 1915. The author finds that the original reference service, begun by George Waterson in 1815, was limited by the lack of trained staff, finances, research collections and adequate facilities.   418

ROTHSTEIN, Samuel. The Development of Reference Services in American Research Libraries. Doctoral dissertation, University of Illinois, 1954. 288 pp., bibl. Published: ALA, 1955.
This study traces the history of reference service in research libraries from its early beginnings around 1875 to the middle of the 20th century. Up to the second decade of the 20th century little actual reference work was being done. Dr. Rothstein cites several reasons for this fact. First, scholars felt the librarians' duty to be one of acquisitions rather than service, and at the same time felt little need for help in their research. Second, little aid was given to students and other inexperienced users, for the philosophy of that period was one of encouraging user independence. After 1940 the ever-increasing flow of literature in all research fields contributed to the researcher's need for assistance in his work. This factor has led to the firm establishment of the reference function in the American research library.   419

THOMPSON, Madeline Cord. History of the Reference Department of the University of Illinois Library. Master's thesis, University of Illinois, 1942. 175 pp., bibl.

This paper presents the history of the development and services of the Reference Department starting from 1897, when the first library building was erected on the campus, the first trained librarian was hired, and the Reference Department was organized. It goes through the year 1940, which marked the end of Phineas L. Windsor's career as Director of the University of Illinois library.   420

Library Education

General Studies.

CAMPBELL, Rosemae Wells. The Development of Public School Librarianship in the United States. Master's thesis, Colorado College, 1953. 67 pp., bibl.
The first school libraries grew out of small classroom libraries, many of them on loan from public libraries. It was not until 1896, when Melvil Dewey pushed for a library department within the N. E. A., that much progress was made. The first professional school librarian was appointed in 1900, and after 1923 school libraries gained a firm footing in America. The author traces the development of quarters, standards and training of school librarians. She also considers the influence of such men as Melvil Dewey, C. C. Certain, and C. C. Williamson. 421

CAMPION, Anna Louise. Education for Special Librarians in the United States and Canada in 1946 and 1952. Master's thesis, Drexel Institute of Technology, 1953. 37 pp., bibl.
The author examined the catalogs of 35 accredited library schools to establish developments in the education of special librarians between 1946 and 1952. She finds a definite trend toward the offering of specific courses in special librarianship. The lack of an adequate teaching literature, facilities and faculties are cited as problems that have confronted library schools in this area of library education.   422

DAUGHTREY, Joyce Alethia. A Content Analysis of Periodical Literature Relating to the Certification of Librarians, 1906 to 1952. Master's thesis, Atlanta University, 1954. 117 pp., bibl.
The first 30 pages of this study present a history of the certification of librarians as evidenced through the literature from 1906 to 1952. The author finds that the first move toward certification of librarians came in 1906, when the Minnesota Public Library Commission issued state certificates on the basis of state examinations. The American Library Association did not take much interest in the problem until after Williamson's groundbreaking report

in 1923, but from that time on the interest in certification grew. In 1952, 22 states had legal certification; 10 had voluntary certification of librarians, and 15 had no specific certification requirements. The author finds that certification has been confined mainly to secondary school librarians. There has been little emphasis on public librarians, almost none on academic librarians. Appendix A is a chronological list of periodical literature on the certification of librarians, 1906 to 1952.   423

EMERT, Florence A. Trends in Thought on the Training of Special Librarians from the Beginning of the Special Libraries Association in 1909 Through 1950. Master's thesis, Western Reserve, 1952. 55 pp., bibl.
After tracing the early history of the Special Libraries Association, this paper considers chronologically the development of a philosophy of education for special librarianship. The author finds it hard to chart a distinct trend, for the period under study has been marked by considerable controversy. The value of a regular library school course for special librarians, and the value of subject specialization over knowledge of library techniques and philosophy were two of the major areas of conflict. The author notes that after 1939 there seemed to be some agreement on the part of leading special librarians that library school training is acceptable if several special library courses are introduced.   424

FLEISCHER, Mary Beth. Credentials Awarded Through August, 1961, by Agencies Presently or Formerly Approved or Accredited by the American Library Association. Master's thesis, University of Texas, 1963. 60 pp., bibl.
The author identifies the credentials (i.e. degrees) in library science that have been employed by agencies for library education in the United States and Canada from 1887 through August of 1961. She also provides information on the type and number of degrees awarded by each of the agencies now or at one time accredited by the American Library Association. Some 50,000 certificates and degrees have been awarded, 28.5 percent of them during the period 1952-1961. Roughly 60 percent of the total were bachelor's degrees (mostly fifth year), nearly 30 percent were master's degrees, 11.5 percent were certificates. Less than one-half of one percent were doctor's degrees.   425

LOHRER, Mary A. Teacher-Librarian Training Program, 1900-1944. Master's thesis, University of Chicago, 1944. 148 pp., bibl. Not examined.   426

SINGLETON, Mildred E. Reference Teaching in the Pioneer

Library Schools, 1883-1903. Master's thesis, Columbia
University, 1942. 195 pp. , bibl.
Studies reference teaching in four pioneer library schools,
those at Columbia, Pratt Institute in Brooklyn, Drexel Institute in Philadelphia, and Armour Institute in Chicago.
Discusses the factors stimulating the development of reference services, and therefore influential in the development of reference teaching. The author finds an extensive
growth in the scope and depth of reference courses in the
four library schools. The major reasons for this growth
are cited as: (1) the changing emphasis in library work
from storage to use; (2) the ever-increasing number of
reference books; and (3) increased use of library collections. The influence of great reference teachers was also
significant.   427
VANN, Sarah K. Training for Librarianship Before 1923, or
prior to the Publication of Williamson's Report on "Training for Library Service." Doctoral dissertation, University of Chicago, 1959. 374 pp. , bibl. Published: ALA, 1961.
Presents a detailed analysis of the ideas and concepts of
library education that evolved during the "Dewey to Williamson" period, 1887-1923. The author finds that too
little attention has been paid to that period, which begins
with the founding of the Library School at Columbia and
ends with the publication of Williamson's report on library
education. She argues that the ideas expressed by Williamson, and those frequently identified with him, had actually
been quite common throughout the years after the establishment of Dewey's school.   428
WICKIZER, A. F. Education for Librarianship; A Brief History 1886-1953. Master's thesis, Western Reserve, 1953.
88 pp. Not examined.   429

Individual Library Schools Arranged by State.

Georgia

CALLAHAN, Betty E. The Carnegie Library School of Atlanta,
1905-1925. Master's thesis, Emory University, 1961. 94
pp. , bibl.
Traces the origins, purposes, content and instructional
approach of the Carnegie Library School of Atlanta. Established in 1905, the Library School became affiliated
in 1925 with Emory University and later developed into
the Emory University Division of Librarianship. The
school was originally a staff training ground for the Carnegie Library of Atlanta, and the public library needs
provided the major influence on curriculum development.

The author finds that the school faced constant problems and did not reach maturity until its affiliation with Emory University. 430

North Carolina

ORR, Adriana Pannevis. A History and Analysis of the Freshman Library Instruction Program Presented at the University of North Carolina. Master's thesis, University of North Carolina, 1958. 94 pp., bibl. Published: ACRL Microcard #125.
The author devotes the first quarter of this paper to a discussion of the reports and correspondence of the Reference Librarian and other university personnel concerned with the establishment of a library orientation program. The program grew out of the library staff's frustration over the poor orientation being given freshmen by the English Department in the 1930's, but the library's program was not formally established until 1948. 431

WING, Mary Jane. A History of the School of Library Science of the University of North Carolina: The First Twenty-five Years. Master's thesis, University of North Carolina, 1958. 150 pp., bibl. Published: ACRL Microcard #119.
Traces the history of the University of North Carolina Library School from 1931 to 1956. Curriculum development, the transition from undergraduate work to graduate work, efforts to win accreditation, and the school's influence on southern and national librarianship are all topics discussed by the author. By 1956 the school had awarded 749 degrees. 432

Ohio

DAVENPORT, Frederick B. A History of the Western Reserve University Library School, 1904-1954. Master's thesis, Western Reserve, 1956. 43 pp., bibl.
This study is concerned with the growth of the institution and devotes little space to the influence of various personalities on the school's development. Seven major chapters deal with: (1) requirements for admission; (2) tuition and expenses; (3) general curriculum; (4) work with children and young people; (5) building and books; (6) the summer school; and (7) certificates and degrees. Appendix E compares entrance requirements at three library schools in 1920. 433

Pennsylvania

NEHLIG, Mary E. The History and Development of the Drexel
Institute Library School, 1892-1914. Master's thesis,
Drexel Institute of Technology, 1952. 48 pp., bibl.
This paper traces the development from 1892 to 1914 of
the third oldest library school in the United States. The
origins of the school, its curriculum, the faculty and
their achievements are all discussed by the author. Special
emphasis is placed on the period 1913-1914, the last year
the school was open until 1922. The school, under the direction of Alice Bertha Kroeger (1892-1909), June Richardson Donnelly (1910-1913), and Corinne Bacon (1913-1914),
had graduated 317 students, two of them men, by 1914. 434

OSBURN, Harriet. A History of the Library Science Department of the Millersville State Teachers College, Millersville, Pennsylvania. Master's thesis, Drexel Institute of
Technology, 1955. 56 pp., bibl.
After briefly surveying the school library situation in Pennsylvania prior to 1921, the author traces the development
of the teacher-librarian curriculum at Millersville State
from its beginnings in the fall of 1922 to June, 1955. The
original program required 15 hours, but had grown to 20
by 1955. Graduates of the school are certified by the State
Department of Public Instruction to serve in the schools
of Pennsylvania. 435

STANBERY, George W., II. History of the Carnegie Library
School; Through Its First Fifty Years. Master's thesis,
Carnegie Institute, 1951. 83 pp., bibl.
Covers the history of the Carnegie Library School from
its beginnings in 1901 through the 1950-1951 session. In
1901 Miss Frances Jenkins Olcott organized the Training
School for Children's Librarians, which in 1916 became a
department of the Carnegie Institute and was renamed the
Carnegie Library School. In 1948 the school started its
one-year post-B.A. program, which led to a Master of Library Science degree. Short biographical sketches of Frances Olcott, Sara Bogle, Lucy Fay, Nina Brotherton and
Elizabeth Nesbitt are included. 436

Texas

ADRIAN, Janet M. A History of the Library Science Department of East Texas State College. Master's thesis, East
Texas State, 1959. 60 pp., bibl.
This paper is a chronological history of the Library Science Department at East Texas State College from 1947
to 1959. In 1947 the Department began offering a major
in library science. One teacher taught all of the classes
and 14 students enrolled in the program. From that time

up to 1959 the Library Science Department awarded 38 Bachelor of Science in Library Science degrees, and 58 Master of Library Science degrees. An appendix contains a list of the recipients and their degrees.   437

WEBB, David A. Local Efforts to Prepare Library Assistants and Librarians in Texas from 1900 to 1942. Doctoral dissertation, University of Chicago, 1963. 356 pp., bibl.
In this study of library education, the author sets the stage by tracing the history of libraries in Texas from 1900 to 1942. Dr. Webb finds that Texas was at least 30 years behind in establishing formal academic programs for the preparation of librarians. It was not until 1919 that the University of Texas opened its library school. 438

Library Associations

Studies Arranged by Subject.

American Association of Law Libraries

McGREGOR, J. W. History of the American Association of Law Libraries from 1906 to 1942. Master's thesis, University of Chicago, 1963. 160 pp., bibl. Not examined.   439

American Library Association

ELLIOTT, Ella M. Federal Relations of the American Library Association, 1930-1940. Master's thesis, University of Chicago, 1946. 75 pp., bibl.
The relationship between libraries and the federal government, which began in 1816 with the exemption of libraries from import duties on books, is studied here. The author emphasizes the period 1930-1940, when the A. L. A. was actively involved with the federal government. Most efforts were aimed at securing advantages for libraries, but the lack of a coordinated A. L. A. program hampered the efficiency of the work. Three appendices are included: (1) a list of A. L. A. boards and committees involved in Federal relations, 1930-1940; (2) a list of statements by A. L. A. representatives at hearings on copyright bills; and (3) a list of A. L. A. activities related to the Federal Government, 1930-1940.   440

American Merchant Marine Library Association

MICHELSON, Aaron I. The American Merchant Marine Library Association--Its History and Functions. Master's thesis, Western Reserve, 1950. 53 pp., bibl.

The American Merchant Marine Library Association was
established by Mrs. Henry Howard in 1921. Its origin was
prompted by the American Library Association, which had
supplied free books to seamen aboard American vessels
during World War I. The A. L. A. transferred to the Association some 65,000 volumes and about $5,000 in unex-
pended funds. In 1924 over 180,000 books were circulated
by the Association. In the next decade financial difficulties
struck the Association and in 1937 only 163 books were
circulated. During World War II circulation jumped great-
ly--768,500 books and 1,500,000 magazines were distribut-
ed to 3,874 ships in 1945.   441

Catholic Library Association

DUNLEAVY, Sister Consolata Maria. The History of the Catholic Library Association, 1921-1961. Master's thesis,
Catholic University of America, 1964. 130 pp., bibl.
This study is mainly concerned with an analysis of the
achievements of the Catholic Library Association. The author lists five major characteristics that have lead to the
independent and progressive nature of the Catholic Library
Association: (1) the foresight and zeal of the founding
fathers; (2) interest and initiative of later executives; (3)
organization and cooperation; (4) well-planned publications
and activities; and (5) a constitution and by-laws that were
revisable and expandable. The author lists in appendices
the presidents and many other officals of C. L. A.   442

District of Columbia Library Association

SEABROOK, Martha. A History of the District of Columbia
Library Association, 1894-1954. Master's thesis, Catholic
University, 1957. 128 pp., bibl.
Traces the history of the Association from its founding in
1894 as the Washington Librarians' Club, with 23 members, to 1954. One of the original founders of the group
was A. R. Spofford, the librarian of Congress. The author describes the D. C. L. A.'s development from 1898,
with emphasis on its activities, publications, and relations
with the A. L. A. A chronological list of D. C. L. A. publications from 1894 through 1954 is included.   443

Medical Library Association

MAGGETTI, Mary T. The Medical Library Association: Its
History and Activities, 1898-1953. Master's thesis, Drexel
Institute of Technology, 1955. 43 pp., bibl.

Traces briefly the history of the Association from its
founding in 1898 up to the year 1953, including a review
of its activities. Special emphasis is placed on the Medical Library Exchange and on the Association's efforts to
develop standardization and certification for medical libraries. The author did not examine the Association's
records.   444

Michigan Ladies' Library Association

HAMNER, Phyllis Norris. The Ladies' Library Association of
Michigan: A Curious Byway in Library History. Master's
thesis, Western Reserve, 1954. 43 pp. , bibl.
This study, not intended as a history of individual libraries, traces the development and achievements of the Ladies' Library Association 1851-1880. Over 44 libraries were
established by the ladies during the 30 years. Many of
them were highly successful in providing library service
to their communities and many continued to serve for over
100 years. Organized by groups of local women, they were
usually subscription libraries open to the public for a
small fee. Appendix II contains excerpts illustrating the
philosophy of service held by each of 26 of the Michigan
Ladies' Library Associations. This study also contains a
chronological list of the 44 libraries according to their
dates of establishment.   445

Music Library Association

BENNETT, Janice Paula. The Music Library Association
1931-1956. Master's thesis, Western Reserve, 1957. 23
pp. , bibl.
This paper brings together all available material on the
Music Library Association and its influence on music librarianship in America. Founded in 1931, at the instiga-
tion of Dr. Carleton Sprague Smith of the New York Public Library, the Music Library Association had grown to
nearly 900 members in 1956. The author surveys noted
activities and projects of the Association, such as its
Checklist of Thematic Catalogues. Important MLA publications, such as the List of Subject Headings, Code for
Cataloging and the official periodical Notes, are also discussed.   446

Southwestern Library Association

WALKER, Mary J. D. The Southwestern Library Association,
1922-1954. Master's thesis, University of Texas, 1959.

222 pp. , bibl.
Describes the development of the Association from its establishment in 1922 through 1954. Emphasis is placed on description and analysis of the factors that contributed to its formulation, administration, activities, and problems. Little attention is devoted to the contributions of individual leaders in the Association.   447

Special Libraries Association - Rio Grande Chapter

HENDRICKSON, Ruth Maria. The Rio Grande Chapter of the Special Libraries Association. Master's thesis, University of Texas, 1962. 72 pp. , bibl.
The first several chapters of this paper deal with the events that led to the organization of the Rio Grande Chapter in 1956. The author finds that the major stimulus was the establishment and expansion of government libraries in New Mexico following World War II. The concomitant increase in research placed greater demands on these small libraries, and the other libraries of the state held little promise of being able to help. The librarians banded together in a special library association to discuss their particular problems and to develop means of cooperation. The chapter was officially recognized in 1956, becoming the 31st member of the Special Libraries Association. 448

Tennessee Library Association

EASTERLY, Ambrose. The Tennessee Library Association's First Fifty Years, 1902-1951. Master's thesis, George Peabody College for Teachers, 1954. 119 pp. , bibl.
The author is concerned with the history of the Tennessee Library Association from its beginnings in 1902 up through 1951. Consideration is given to an analysis of the Association's beginnings and objectives and to its accomplishments. The paper also contains a directory of annual meetings and lists of officers. It concludes with recommendations for increasing the T. L. A.'s effectiveness as a professional association.   449

Texas Library Association

KELL, Beatrice Fineman. An Analysis of Texas Library Association Membership and Officers, 1902-1956. Master's thesis, University of Texas, 1956. 133 pp. , bibl.
This study is concerned with an analysis and interpretation of (1) factual changes in membership of the Texas Library Association; (2) changes in the status of the divisional

members; and (3) the pattern of office-holding and membership representation 1902-1956. The author finds that as the Texas Library Association grew, the direction and determination of its policy shifted from the membership as a whole to a selective Executive Board, and that there often tended to be little communication between the Board and the members. At the same time, the development of special interest groups or divisions within the Texas Library Association created competition for posts on the Executive Board. 450

Teen-Age Library Association, Texas

McLAREN, D. N. First Ten Years of the Teen-Age Library Association of Texas, 1949-1959. Master's thesis, University of Texas, 1961. 66 pp. Not examined. 451

Biographies of Librarians and Library Benefactors Arranged by Subject

Blue, Thomas Fountain.

WRIGHT, Lillian Taylor. Thomas Fountain Blue, Pioneer Librarian, 1866-1935. Master's thesis, Atlanta University, 1955. 59 pp., bibl.
Thomas Fountain Blue was one of the first Negro library leaders. In 1905 he was named head of the colored branch of the Louisville Free Public Library. From then until 1935 he provided leadership for his own library and also contributed to branch library development in this country. He pioneered in the apprentice training of Negro library assistants and was one of the first organizers of Negro librarians. 452

Bostwick, Arthur Elmore.

CUNNINGHAM, Larry Lee. Contributions of Arthur Elmore Bostwick to the Library Profession. Master's thesis, Indiana University, 1962. 95 pp., bibl.
Dr. Bostwick is recognized as one of the outstanding figures in American library history and this study aims at pinpointing his ideas on library science and their influence on the development of American librarianship. Dr. Bostwick was director of the St. Louis Public Library from 1909 to 1938; the author of numerous books, the most important of which was The American Public Library; president of several state library associations and

the American Library Association; and a member of the editorial staff of such reference works as the Funk and Wagnalls Standard Dictionary. The author includes a brief biography of Dr. Bostwick and a bibliography of his published works.   453

Buffington, Willie Lee.

CARR, Louise Douglas. The Reverend Willie Lee Buffington's Life and Contributions to the Development of Rural Libraries in the South. Master's thesis, Atlanta University, 1958. 53 pp., bibl.
In 1931 Reverend Buffington decided to ask for donations of books for Negro pupils in the South. Since his total assets were 10 cents, he was able to mail an appeal to only five people. One person, the Rev. Lorenzo H. King of New York, responded, and several months later over 1,000 books arrived in barrels. There were more than were needed for a school library, so the Rev. Buffington decided to build a public library. With help from the residents of Edgefield, South Carolina, on December 31, 1932 the first of his Faith Cabin Libraries was opened. He went on to establish 26 more libraries in South Carolina and 55 in Georgia. The total number of volumes was over 200,000.   454

Butler, Susan Dart.

BOLDEN, Ethel Evangeline Martin. Susan Dart Butler--Pioneer Librarian. Master's thesis, Atlanta University, 1959. 31 pp., bibl.
Susan Dart Butler, aware of the deficiencies in public library service for Negroes in the South, was instrumental in getting financial assistance from the Julius Rosewald Fund to aid in the establishment of a library for Negroes in Charleston, North Carolina. In 1931 the library was opened and from that date until 1957 she served as its librarian. In 1952 the library, called the Dart Hall Branch Library, circulated some 150,000 volumes. This paper describes her efforts to improve library service to Negroes in Charleston.   455

Cutter, Charles Ammi.

LITTLE, Agnes Eastman. Charles Ammi Cutter, Librarian at Forbes Library, Northampton, Massachusetts, 1894-1903. Master's thesis, University of North Carolina, 1962. 52 pp., bibl.

This biography of Charles Ammi Cutter, one of the greatest American librarians, covers his career as Director of the Forbes Library in Northampton from 1894 to 1903. The author feels that these years were the most personally rewarding of Cutter's life. The four chapters of this paper provide (1) a brief historical sketch of Northampton; (2) a discussion of the activities and writings of Cutter before he joined the Forbes Library in 1894; (3) Cutter's theories of library management as seen through his administration of the Forbes Library; and (4) a summary of his work at Forbes.   456

MORSE, Clarence Ralph. A Biographical, Bibliographical Study of Charles Ammi Cutter, Librarian. Master's thesis, University of Washington, 1961. 98 pp., bibl.
The first part of this study briefly traces Cutter's life from his birth in 1837 to his death in 1903. Cutter was librarian of the Boston Athenaeum for 25 years, and later he was Director of Forbes Library at Northampton. The second part of this paper is a chronological listing of some 100 articles by Cutter that appeared in The Nation and the North American Review. All of the articles (90) in The Nation and three of the North American Review articles are annotated.   457

Davis, Raymond Cazallis.

ABBOTT, John Cushman. Raymond Cazallis Davis and the University of Michigan General Library, 1877-1905. Doctoral dissertation, University of Michigan, 1957. 315 pp., bibl. (D. A. 58-1370)
The first part of Dr. Abbott's study is devoted to Davis' life, from his birth in 1836 until his death in 1919. In 1868 he was named Assistant Librarian at the University of Michigan and in 1877 he was named Head Librarian. Part two is a history of the library during Davis' reign as director, 1877-1905. Davis was faced with numerous difficulties, most serious of which were a lack of funds and problems with the catalog. His interest in public services prompted him to institute a credit course in bibliography (the first in this country) in 1883.   458

Eastman, Linda Anne.

PHILLIPS, C. O. Linda Anne Eastman; Librarian. Master's thesis, Western Reserve, 1953. 46 pp., bibl. Not examined.   459

WRIGHT, Alice Edwards. Linda A. Eastman: Pioneer in Librarianship. Master's thesis, Kent State University, 1952.

83 pp., bibl.
This biography of Linda A. Eastman emphasizes her pioneering efforts on behalf of American librarianship. Miss Eastman served the profession for 43 years. From 1918 to 1938 she was librarian of the Cleveland Public Library. The author devotes chapters to three areas where Miss Eastman's influence was great: work with the blind, divisional plans in libraries, and adult education.   460

Evans, Charles.

HOLLEY, Edward G. Charles Evans: American Bibliographer. Doctoral dissertation, University of Illinois, 1961. 593 pp., bibl. Published: University of Illinois Press, 1963.
The first part of this study deals with Evans the librarian. After working under W. F. Poole at the Boston Athenaeum, Evans became Director of the Indianapolis Public Library when he was only 22. Dr. Holley traces Evans' frustrating library career from that time until 1901, when he was dismissed from his library post at the Chicago Historical Society and decided to devote the rest of his life to his American Bibliography. Evans was one of the founders of the American Library Association in 1876, and in 1877 he attended the first International Conference of Librarians in London. The second part of this study deals with his career as a bibliographer.   461

Foik, Paul J.

BRESIE, Mayellen. Paul J. Foik, C.S.C. Librarian and Historian. Master's thesis, University of Texas, 1964. 168 pp., bibl.
After briefly sketching Father Foik's early life and education, from his birth in 1879 to 1912, the author deals with his library career. From 1912 to 1924 he served as librarian at Notre Dame, and from 1924 to 1941 he served as librarian at St. Edward's University in Austin, Texas. Father Foik's leadership in establishing the Catholic Library Association, the initiation of the Catholic Periodical Index, and his many activities as a Catholic historian are also discussed. A bibliography of his extensive writings is included (pp. 152-157).   462

Franklin, Benjamin.

KORTY, Margaret Barton. Benjamin Franklin and Eighteenth-Century American Libraries. Master's thesis, Catholic University, 1964. 244 pp., bibl. Published: Transactions

of the American Philosophical Society (New Series), 55(9):82.
1965, and Journal of Library History II (1967), 271-328.
Describes Franklin's extensive influence on American library development, which began with his establishment of
America's first social library in 1731. Besides describing
Franklin's efforts on behalf of the Library Company of
Philadelphia, the author analyzes his many other library
activities, such as: (1) trustee of the Loganian Library;
(2) contributor to the libraries of Harvard and Yale; (3)
founder of the American Philosophical Society and build-
er of its library collections; (4) a founder of the Pennsylvania Hospital, home of the first Medical Library in America; and (5) contributor of a library to the town of Franklin, Massachusetts, which eventually evolved into the town's
public library.   463

Graham, Bessie.

CAMPBELL, Mildred Melsheimer. Bessie Graham, Bibli-
ophile. Master's thesis, Texas State College for Women,
1953. 71 pp., bibl.
Bessie Graham is familiar to all librarians as the author
of the Bookman's Manual. This paper is divided into two
major sections, a biographical study and a chronological
analysis of her writings. Bessie Graham attended the
Drexel Library School in 1910, and in 1914 she began
teaching a course "about books" in the William Penn
Evening School. She later taught courses in bibliography
at the New York Public Library. She published the first
edition of the Bookman's Manual in 1921, the same year
she became librarian of the Apprentice's Library of
Philadelphia. She resigned in 1924 to go to Temple University as head of the Library Science Department, remaining there until 1940. A bibliography of her extensive
writings is included in this paper.   464

Grothaus, Julia.

DRUMMOND, Donald Ryan. Julia Grothaus, San Antonio Librarian. Master's thesis, University of Texas, 1964. 100
pp., bibl.
The author traces the life of Miss Grothaus from her
birth, through high school, to college at Southwest Texas
State Normal School, the University of Tennessee, and
the University of Illinois Library School. In 1922 she was
named assistant librarian at the San Antonio Public Library, and in 1933 she became its director, a position she
held for over 20 years. She instituted many new services

there: the first bookmobile service in the city, the first
integrated library service, in-service training for librarians, and an audio-visual department. The author describes her many difficulties with local censors and her cour-
ageous defense of the freedom to read in San Antonio.
She was an influential member of numerous library associations and served as president of the Texas Library Association 1940-1941.   465

Gunter, Lillian.

NICHOLS, Margaret Irby. Lillian Gunter: Pioneer Texas County Librarian, 1870-1926. Master's thesis, University of
Texas, 1958. 81 pp. , bibl.
Lillian Gunter was a leader of Texas librarians from 1914
to 1926. She began her career by transforming a small
subscription library into the Gainsville Public Library,
which she directed for 10 years. She became interested
in rural library service and in 1915 drafted the County
Free Library Bill. The bill proved ineffective, and in
1919 she fought successfully for its amendment. This success remains her greatest achievement. In 1920 she established and directed the Cooke County Library. She was
active in the Texas Library Association and was a co-
founder of the Southwestern Library Association. This
study emphasizes her efforts to establish good rural library service in Texas. The author had access to the
Gunter papers in the Texas State Historical Museum and
to the "Gunter Diary, " autobiographical memoirs written
by Miss Gunter, 1921-1924, located in the State Archives,
Austin.   466

Hewins, Caroline Maria.

DEKENIS, Alma. Caroline Maria Hewins: Pioneer in the Development of Library Service for Children. Master's thesis, New Haven State Teachers College, 1959. 58 pp. , bibl.
Caroline Hewins joined the library profession at a time
when library service for children was in its developmental
stages. Her first library job brought her under the tute-
lage of William F. Poole at the Boston Athenaeum. In
1875 she became librarian of the Young Men's Institute of
Hartford, Connecticut, and served there for some 50 years.
Her special interest from the very beginning was library
work with children. She bought good children's books, encouraged the young to use the library, and provided inex-
pensive memberships to the local schools. In 1893 the library became the Hartford Public Library, and in 1904

she persuaded city officials to provide a separate children's room. A founder of the Connecticut Library Association in 1891, she was recognized as a national leader in the field of children's librarianship. Her most noted contributions were in the area of bibliography of children's reading, but she was also a prolific and influential writer and contributed many papers to the professional journals. This paper contains "Books, Pamphlets and Articles by Caroline M. Hewins." pp., 55-58.   467

Hoole, William Stanley.

HOOLE, Martha Dubose. William Stanley Hoole, Student-Teacher-Librarian-Author. Master's thesis, Florida State University, 1958. 78 pp., bibl.
The author treats her subject in two parts. The first is a biography, while the second is an analysis of Mr. Hoole's written contributions. Hoole was born in 1903, was graduated from Wofford College, South Carolina, in 1924, and began teaching high school English the same year. In 1934 he earned a doctor's degree from Duke University. In 1935 he became Director of the Phillips Library at Birmingham-Southern College in Alabama. From 1937 to 1939 he served as head of the Baylor University Library. In 1939 he became librarian and Director of the Department of Library Service at North Texas State College. In 1944 he was named Director of Libraries at the University of Alabama. Dr. Hoole is one of the most published librarians. History, literature, the theatre, and library science are all topics of interest to him. A list of his extensive writings is included (pp. 58-76).   468

Lowe, John Adams.

O'FLYNN, Mary Ellen. John Adams Lowe; Administrative and Library Planner. Master's thesis, Drexel Institute of Technology, 1955. 59 pp., Not examined.   469

McDiarmid, Errett Weir.

McCULLEY, Kathleen Mary. Dr. Errett Weir McDiarmid's Application of His Philosphy of Library Administration in the University of Minnesota Library, 1943-1951. Master's thesis, University of North Carolina, 1963. 84 pp., bibl.
This study of Dr. E. W. McDiamid, librarian at the University of Minnesota and later Dean of the College of Science, Literature and the Arts at the University of Minnesota, is an effort to ascertain how he introduced and

carried out his philosophy of library administration. His philosophy is drawn from his many publications and includes the methods he advocated. No attempt is made at critical analysis, but the author attempts to show how an experienced library administrator must have a definable and flexible philosophy to do his job correctly.   470

Moore, Anne Carroll.

AKERS, Nancy Meade. Anne Carroll Moore; A Study of Her Work with Children's Libraries and Literature. Master's thesis, Pratt Institute, 1951. 49 pp., bibl.
Anne Carroll Moore, a pioneer in children's library work, became in 1896 the first children's librarian at the Pratt Institute Free Library in Brooklyn. Ten years later she became the first superintendent of work with children at the New York Public Library. Miss Moore remained there for 45 years and through example and published writings greatly influenced the development of children's work in America. The author of this paper presents a chronological history of Miss Moore's efforts and contributions. A bibliography of her publications on librarianship is included (pp. 48-49).   471

Monti, Minnie Sweet.

HERSHEY, Frederick Earnshaw. Minnie Sweet Monti: Her Life and Influence. Master's thesis, Western Reserve, 1957. 41 pp., bibl.
This study traces Minnie Sweet Monti's life from her birth on March 22, 1888, to her retirement as order librarian at the Cleveland Public Library in 1956. She was graduated from Western Reserve University in 1908 and then joined the order department at the Cleveland Public Library. In 1950 she was named head of the order department. This paper deals mainly with her labors at Cleveland.   472

Ohio State Librarians.

COHEN, Sidney. Biographical Data on the Librarians of the Ohio State Library, 1817-1960. Master's thesis, Kent State University, 1961. 120 pp.
This paper contains short biographical sketches of the 28 librarians who have served the Ohio State Library.   473

Owen, Thomas McAdory.
KETCHERSID, Arthur Lloyd. Thomas McAdory Owen: Archivist.

Master's thesis, Florida State University, 1961. 77 pp.,
bibl.
Thomas M. Owen died in 1920, but his pioneering efforts
in archive organization and development are still recognized as highly authoritative. The author traces his life, with
special emphasis on his efforts on behalf of historical archives in the South. His major achievement came in the
creation and development of the Albama Department of
Archives and History. This department set a pattern for
archival organization that has been copied extensively
throughout the nation.   474

Pearson, Edmund Lester.

HYLAND, Laura. An Interpretation of Edmund Lester Pear-
son--Librarian Extraordinary, to Which Is Added a Bibliography of His Works. Master's thesis, Carnegie Institute
of Technology, 1952. 62 pp., bibl.
This study of Edmund Lester Pearson, librarian, bookman,
mystery writer, and wit, places emphasis on Pearson the
bookman and author. Pearson never made a great dent on
the American library profession, but he was one of those
wonderful, rare types who loved books, read them, wrote
them, reviewed them--in short, lived them. His Old Librarians' Almanac stands as one of the wittiest spoofs
on librarianship ever written. Pearson liked to laugh at
the "old librarians" and garnered considerable enmity in
the process. The author includes a bibliography of Pearson's work (pp. 41-62).   475

Poole, William Frederick.

WILLIAMSON, William Landram. William Frederick Poole
and the Modern Library Movement. Doctoral dissertation,
University of Chicago, 1959. 2 volumes, bibl. Published:
New York - Columbia University Press, 1963.
When the idea of the public library began to develop in
the latter half of the 19th century, one man stood out as
the acknowledged leader--William Frederick Poole, a pioneer and a highly influential American librarian. Poole's
library career led him from the Boston Athenaeum, 1856-
1868, to the directorship of the Cincinnati Public Library,
1896-1873, to the first directorship of the new Chicago
Public Library, 1874-1886, and finally to the directorship
of the Newberry Library in Chicago, 1887-1894. Poole
was a recognized historian as well as a leading librarian.
His most significant publication was Poole's Index to Periodical Literature, a forerunner of the Readers' Guide.

Poole also served as president of the American Library
Association and the American Historical Association. 476

Power, Effie Louise.

BECKER, Margaret B. Effie Louise Power: Pioneer in the Development of Library Services for Children. Master's thesis, Western Reserve, 1950. 76 pp., bibl.
In the first three chapters the author surveys library service to children before 1900, traces the early history of
public library service to children at the Cleveland Public
Library, and analyzes work with children as it was presented at the annual meetings of the American Library
Association from 1889 to 1906. The next four chapters
deal with Miss Power's pioneer contributions in the varied
facets of her career: (1) as supervisor of children's work,
St. Louis Public, 1911-1914; (2) as head of the Children's
Department, Carnegie Library, Pittsburgh, 1914-1920; (3)
as director of work with children, Cleveland Public Library, 1920-1937; and (4) as author, bibliographer and
compiler. A bibliography of her published work is included (pp. 74-76). 477

Richardson, Ernest Cushing.

BRANSCOMB, Lewis Capers, Jr. A Bio-bibliographic Study of
Ernest Cushing Richardson, 1860-1939. Doctoral dissertation, University of Chicago, 1954. 143 pp., bibl.
Dr. Bronscomb traces Richardson's life from his birth in
1860 to his education at Amherst, and from there through
his professional career. Beginning as librarian at the
Hartford Theological Seminary, Princeton, he became finally a bibliography consultant at the Library of Congress.
Richardson was able to exert much influence through his
personal contacts, made as president of A. L. A. 1904-
1905, as chirman of numerous committees of the American Historical Society, and as vice president, 1906-1909,
of the Bibliographical Society of America. However his
contributions to the professional literature were his greatest legacy. His first paper appeared in 1883 when he was
23 and his last (the 230th) appeared in 1939. His Classification Theoretical and Practical (1901) is highly respected. His work in library history--Beginnings of Libraries
(1914), Biblical Libraries (1914), Some Old Egyptian Librarians (1911)--is still widely read. Dr. Branscomb discusses his writing and provides a bibliography of Richardson's published works. 478

Rogan, Octavia F.

BANKS, K. Octavia F. Rogan, Texas Librarian. Master's
thesis, University of Texas, 1963. 151 pp. Not ex-
amined.   479

Sharp, Katharine.

GROTZINGER, Laurel Ann. The Power and the Dignity: Librarianship and Katharine Sharp. Doctoral dissertation,
University of Illinois, 1964. 375 pp., bibl. Published:
Scarecrow Press, 1966.
This study presents the life of Katharine Sharp, 1865-1914.
Miss Sharp studied under Melvil Dewey and was an influential advocate of his philosophy of library service. The
author first surveys Sharp's early life and education and
then discusses her very significant contributions to library
science. Miss Sharp established and guided the Midwest's
first library school, in Chicago, 1893-1897. She was then
brought to the University of Illinois, where she served as
Director of the Library School and librarian of the University from 1897 to 1906. Her administration of the library
was efficient and forward looking and her influence on library education was immeasurable. It was under her direction that the University of Illinois Library School gained
the first rank in its field, and her personal example
brought new stature to the library profession. In 1907, after working herself to near exhaustion, she resigned to
become vice-president of Dewey's New York Lake Placid
Club.   480

Spofford, Ainsworth Rand.

MILLER, Charles Herbert. Ainsworth Rand Spofford, 1825-
1908. Master's thesis, George Washington University,
1938. Not examined.   481
SCHUBACH, Bernice Woodbury. Ainsworth Rand Spofford and
"The Library of the United States." Master's thesis,
Northern Illinois University, 1965. 133 pp., bibl.
Ainsworth Rand Spofford (1825-1908) served the Library
of Congress for 47 years (1861-1908), 33 of them as Director. From the beginning of his administration there
was a pressing space problem, appropriations were small,
there was a shortage of help to handle the ever-increasing duties of the library, and collection building was moving very slowly. Spofford attacked each problem. He worked for, and got, a new building. He increased the staff
from six to 42 (1861-1896). He tightened the loopholes in

the copyright law, instituted exchanges, and achieved increased appropriations. All this led to a tremendous growth in the size of the library's collection, from 63,000 items in 1861 to around 2,000,000 in 1908. Despite meager budgets Spofford was able to acquire the Peter Force Historical Collection and the Toner Collection, which greatly increased the library's resources. He guided the preparation of the catalog of authors and the index to subjects, and he moved for the distribution of Library of Congress cards, a practice that was formally instituted by his successor, Herbert Putnam.   482

Tyler, Alice Sarah.

RICHARDSON, Cora Ella. Alice Sarah Tyler: A Biographical Study. Master's thesis, Western Reserve, 1951. 43 pp., bibl.
Miss Tyler was one of the leading library educators of the early 20th century. This study divides her life into five major segments: (1) early life, education and first position, 1859-1900; (2) Secretary of the Iowa State Library Commission, 1900-1913; (3) Director and Dean of the School of Library Service at Western Reserve, 1913-1929; (4) library interests and personal life; and (5) active retirement and death, 1929-1944. Miss Tyler served as president of the Ohio Library Association, 1916-1917; president of the Association of American Library Schools, 1918-1919; and president of the American Library Association in 1920. A bibliography of her published works is included (pp. 42-43).   483

Vormelker, Rose L.

MAGNER, Mary Jo. The Businessman's Librarian--Rose L. Vormelker. Master's thesis, Western Reserve, 1957. 106 pp., bibl.
Rose Vormelker is best known for her pioneering efforts toward establishing the Business Information Bureau (BIB) of the Cleveland Public Library. Under her guidance it rapidly became a respected source of business information. This study follows her career through the Detroit Public Library (1919-1922), the Science and Technology Division at the Cleveland Public (1922-1925), the White Motor Company (1925-1928), the BIB (1928-1955), to Assistant Director of the Cleveland Public Library (1955-1956), and finally to the Forest City Publishing Company. A bibliography of her extensive publications is included (pp. 103-105). 484

West, Elizabeth Howard.

HESTER, Goldia Ann. Elizabeth Howard West, Texas Librarian. Master's thesis, University of Texas, 1965. 110 pp.,
bibl.
Elizabeth Howard West was a pioneer Texas librarian
(1873-1948). The most extensive part of this paper is devoted to Miss West's career as a librarian: founder and
president of the Texas Library Association; state librarian and initiator of library service for the blind in Texas;
librarian of the Texas Technical College; and a leader in
the Texas public library field. Succeeding sections describe
the associations she influenced, her publications (library
science, American history, Spanish colonial history), and
her education. The author lists and analyzes her published
works (pp. 93-97). 485

Winsor, Justin.

BOROME, Joseph A. The Life and Letters of Justin Winsor.
Doctoral dissertation, Columbia University, 1950. Not examined. 486

Studies of the Literature of American Librarianship

BLOUGH, Nancy L. Histories of Some Major Library Periodicals. Master's thesis, Western Reserve, 1955. 67 pp.,
bibl.
This study presents brief histories of 16 library periodicals: (1) Booklist; (2) A. L. A. Bulletin; (3) Subscription
Books Bulletin; (4) College and Research Libraries; (5)
Journal of Cataloging and Classification; (6) Serial Slants;
(7) Bulletin of the Medical Library Association; (8) Special
Libraries; (9) Catholic Library World; (10) American Documents; (11) Publishers Weekly; (12) Library Journal; (13)
Wilson Library Bulletin; (14) Horn Book Magazine; (15)
Library Quarterly; and (16) Library Trends. An appendix
lists the publications that index each journal and gives
chronological listings of the editors for each journal. 487
DUNN, Aileen. The Nature and Functions of Readers Advisory Service As Revealed by a Survey of the Literature
of the Field from 1935-1950. Master's thesis, Western Reserve, 1950. 32 pp., bibl.
In the early 1920's the first Readers Advisory Services
were established. A great number of people, feeling that
their education was inadequate, were turning to the library
for further study. Librarians were quick to see the need
for a serious form of guidance for these new readers and

from this recognition came the development of the individualized Readers Advisory Service, which sprang up suddenly all over America during the 20's and 30's. The author finds that this trend has been reversed since the 40's and that many libraries had abandoned their formal attempts at reader guidance by 1950. The author's survey of the literature finds no distinct trend or pattern of change apparent, but rather a highly diversified service with little obvious uniformity. 488

HANKINS, Frank Dale. The Treatment of Basic Problems in the Library Journal, 1900-1930. Master's thesis, University of Texas, 1951. 256 pp., bibl.
To ascertain the basic problems of librarianship from 1900-1930, the author analyzed all issues of the Library Journal for the years 1900, 1910, 1920, and 1930. The author presents, with the aid of many tables, the rising and falling interests of librarians in such issues as bibliographic control, administration, book selection, and the philosophy of librarianship. 489

LANDRAM, Christina Oliver. A Study of the Changing Concept of American Librarians As Reflected in the Novels of the Twentieth Century. Master's thesis, Texas State College, 1951. 93 pp., bibl.
This is an attempt to test the hypothesis that there was a change in the image of the librarian as expressed by 20th-century novelists. To see if the librarians who were portrayed in the early part of the century were different from those portrayed in later years, the author located 36 novels in which a librarian was the major character. The results of this historical survey showed that novelists had pictured librarians as young, attractive, single women in most cases. The greatest changes came in the areas of education, specialized training, interest in the profession and satisfaction in work. 490

MADDOX, Lucy Jane. Trends and Issues in American Librarianship As Reflected in the Papers and Proceedings of the American Library Association, 1876-1885. Doctoral dissertation, University of Michigan, 1958. 590 pp., bibl. (D. A. 58-7763)
The decade from 1876 to 1885 is generally considered the beginning of the modern library movement in America. In this study the author delineates the trends and issues that developed during this period. She finds that the techniques and philosophy of librarianship projected then are still widely accepted, and that few radical departures from that early thinking can be found. During that decade the most discussed library subject was cataloging and classification, and the author reviews the six major systems

developed. Among other significant topics treated are (1) the rise of public library service for adults; (2) library building problems; (3) cooperative ventures; (4) library legislation; and (5) circulation systems. The author also evaluates the contributions of leading librarians during this decade, such as Dewey, Poole, Winsor, Cutter, Green and Sanders.   491

NEAL, P. Library Problems, 1876-1886; An Analysis of "Notes and Queries" in "Library Journal" and "Proceedings of the American Library Association." Master's thesis, Carnegie Institute of Technology, 1954. Not examined.   492

PEIRCE, Patricia. A Study of the Philosophy of Librarianship; A Review of the Relevant Literature, 1930-1950. Master's thesis, Drexel Institute of Technology, 1951. 46 pp., bibl. A historical and critical review of what was written in the professional literature 1930-1950 about the philosophy of librarianship. An extensive bibliography of such writings is included.   493

SPARKS, C. G. Presidential Addresses Made to the American Library Association, 1876-1951: A Content Analysis. Master's thesis, University of Texas, 1952. 162 pp., bibl. Published: ACRL Microcard #131.
This analysis of the major ideas to be found in the presidential addresses to the American Library Association from 1876 to 1951 illustrates the most important issues facing the profession during those years. Such topics as "What a Librarian Should Be" got emphasis before 1930, while most addresses after that year were oriented towards "Libraries and Their Organization." The topic of professional associations was also found to be a frequent subject of presidential addresses.   494

Miscellaneous Studies

BEDDIE, James S. Libraries in the Twentieth Century. Doctoral dissertation, Harvard University, 1928. Not examined.   495

DUCSAY, William Joseph. A Translation of the "History of Libraries in the United States of America" from the Milkau Collection. Master's thesis, Western Reserve, 1959. 160 pp., bibl.
This is a translation of chapter 12, pages 776 to 855, of the second part of the third volume in the Handbuch der Bibliothewissenschaft, published 1952-1957.   496

Author Index
The numbers refer to entry numbers.

Carroll, F. C., 374
Carter, M. A., 17
Chalker, W. J., 394
Chamberlain, L. C., 248
Church, F. L., 230
Clark, R. B. Jr., 102
Clinefeller, R. W., 302
Clopine, J. Jr., 43
Clymer, B. F. Jr., 289
Cochran, M. A., 325
Cody, N. B., 212
Cohen, S., 473
Colla, Sister M. B., 246
Collier, F. G., 44
Collins, L. T., 140
Cook, V. R., 72
Coover, R. W., 396
Copeland, E. F., 175
Corcoran, S. R., 402
Coughlin, B. M., 93
Cowles, L. H., 363
Cramer, J. C., 141
Cranford, J. P., 290
Crittenden, J. L. J., 78
Crook, M. R., 4
Crouch, M. L., 204
Crumpacker, G. F., 96
Cunning, E. T., 312
Cunningham, L. L., 453
Daughtrey, J. A., 423
Davenport, F. B., 433
Davis, E. G., 18
Davis, F. C., 45
Davis, J. M., 116
Day, N. J., 19
Dekenis, A., 467
Diana, J. P., 190
Diaz, A. J., 291
Dickey, P. W., 109
DiPietro, L. N., 191
Ditzion, S. H., 46, 47
Dodge, A. C., 20
Donaldson, L. L., 384
Donley, V. L., 342
Donze, S. L., 142
Drummond, D. R., 465
Ducsay, W. J., 496
Duncan, A. McK., 249

Duncan, R. B., 324
Duniway, D. C., 344
Dunkley, G. C., 388
Dunleavy, Sister C. M., 442
Dunn, A., 488
Earnshaw, T. L., 313
Easterly, A., 449
Eaton, J. D., 292
Eberhart, W. L., 48
Eckert, C. J., 143
Edsall, M. H., 328
Egolf, J. L., 192
Elias, W. D., 144
Elliot, E. M., 440
Elliot, M. E., 218
Emert, F. A., 424
Engley, D. B., 276
Erickson, E. W., 231
Eury, W., 124
Fannin, G. M., 117
Farrow, M. H., 293
Feaster, D. M., 87
Fedder, M. B., 21
Feeney, R. B., 385
Fleischer, M. B., 425
Fleischer, M. L., 146
Flener, J. G., 22
Fonville, E. R., 58
Forney, D. J., 145
Fortin, C. C., 279
Foster, P. M., 390
Freund, C. E., 343
Gallant, E. F., 113
Galloway, M. L., 375
Garrison, B. S., 125
Gates, E. S., 67
Gates, J. K., 63
Gelfand, M. A., 232
Gibson, F. E., 106
Giddings, R. L., 68
Gill, S. G., 75
Gillespie, R. C., 213
Girvin, A. G., 314
Girvin, C. M., 193
Gladeck, A. A., 364
Goldman, S., 354
Goldstein, D., 118
Goock, R. E., 147

172

Waldron, R. K., 349
Walker, M. H., 350
Walker, M. J. D., 447
Walther, L. V. A., 91
Ward, B. A., 225
Webb, D. A., 438
Weis, L. A., 169
Welborn, E. C., 37
Whedbee, M. M., 131
Wheeler, J. T., 9
Whitney, E. M., 200
Wickizer, A. F., 429
Wilcox, H. M., 38
Wilcox, L. E., 257
Wilkins, M. J., 415
Willet, M. M., 416
Williams, Sister M. L., 376
Williamson, W. L., 476
Willis, D. E., 360
Wine, E., 170
Wing, M. J., 432
Winger, A. K., 201
Wofford, A., 383
Wolcott, M. D., 171
Wolf, N. E., 351
Wong, R., 120
Wright, A. E., 460
Wright, L. T., 452
Yenawine, W. S., 258
Yockey, R. M., 185
Young, M. J., 172
Young, S. S., 173
Zimmerman, M., 92

Subject Index
The numbers refer to entry numbers.

86; Story Telling in, 87; and Charles Evans, 461
Industrial Relations Research Libraries, 336

Jackson County Public Library, Ohio, 168
Jefferson, Thomas, classification scheme, 413
Jefferson Medical College Library, Philadelphia, 312
Jewett, Charles Coffin, 407
Johns Hopkins University Library, Medical Library, 271
Johnston County Library System, N. C., 123

Kansas State Teachers College Library, 262
Kemp Public Library, Wichita Falls, Tex., 210
Kent Public Library, Ohio, 155
Ketchiken Public Library, 60
Kittitas County Library, Wash., 220
Knoxville Public Library, 207

La Retama Public Library, Corpus Christi, Tex., 213
La Salle College Library, Philadelphia, Pa., 319
Lafayette College Library, Easton, Pa., 322
Lakewood Public Library, Ohio, 161
Lancaster Social Library, Pa., 30
Land-Grant Colleges, libraries in, 239, 242
Lane Public Library, Hamilton, Ohio, 138
Law Libraries Association, 439
Lee County Public Library, Miss., 110
Legislation, for libraries; in Indiana, 91; in Kansas, 96; in North
    Carolina, 130; in Ohio, 381; Illinois, Wisconsin, Indiana, 369
Leonard Case Library, Cleveland, 301
Lepper Library, Lisbon, Ohio, 151
Lexington, early libraries in, 18
Liberal Arts College Libraries, 241
Librarians, in novels, 490
Library of Congress; reference service, 418; and Ernest C.
    Richardson, 478; and Ainsworth R. Spofford, 481, 482
Library Journal, 489
Lima Public Library, Ohio, 135
Literary Societies, 233, 240; at Hiram College, Ohio, 305, 309
Louisiana, early libraries in, 5
Louisiana State Library, 395
Louisville, University of, Libraries, 263
Louisville Public Library, 452
Lowe, John Adams, 469

McDiarmid, Errett Weir, 470
Mann, Margaret, 406
Maps, cataloging and classification of, 401
Marion County Public Library, Ind., 89

181

Maryland, early libraries in, 9
Maryland State Library, 396
Medical Library Association, 444
Medical Subject Headings, 408, 415
Memphis Public Library, 208
Mentor Public Library, Ohio, 164
Merchant Marine Library Association, 441
Miami Public Library, Fla. , 75
Michigan, Ladies Library Association of, 445
Michigan, University of, Libraries, 278, 458
Middle States Association of Colleges and Secondary Schools,
    evaluation of college and university libraries, 232
Millersville State Teachers College, Library Science Depart-
    ment, 435
Minneapolis, special libraries in, 368
Minneapolis Public Library, 106, 107
Minnesota, University of, Library, 470
Mississippi, University of, Library, 282
Missouri, University of, Library, 283
Monessen Public Library, Pa. , 189
Monti, Minnie Sweet, 472
Moore, Anne Carroll, 471
Morgan State College Library, Md. , 274
Mount Vernon Public Library, Ohio, 153
Music Library Association, 446

Napoleon Public Library, Ohio, 159
Nashville Public Library, 209
Nassau County Library Association Union Catalog, N. Y. , 416
Negroes, Library service to, 40, 41; in Bessemer, Ala. , 58; in
    Montgomery, Ala. , 59; in Atlanta, 77; in Columbus, Ga. ,
    78; in Macon, Ga. , 81; in Jackson, Miss. , 109; in Salisbury,
    N. C. , 121; in Winston-Salem, N. C. , 127; in Knoxville, 207;
    in Memphis, 208; in Nashville, 209; in Galveston, 211; in
    Charleston, 455
New Britain Institute Library, Conn. , 363
New Mexico State Library, 397
Newark Library Association, 32
New York Herald Tribune Library, 337
New York Public Library; circulation department, 53; traveling
    library, 114; story hour, 117; service to the blind, 118;
    Chatham Square Branch, 120; Catalog of the Schomberg Col-
    lection, 403; and Anne Carroll Moore, 471
New York State Library, 398
Newberry Library, 476
Newspaper Libraries, 337
Newtown, Pa. , social library in, 31
Normal School Libraries, 230

182

Norristown Public Library, Pa., 200
North Carolina Agricultural and Technical College Library, 298
North Carolina Library Association, 122
North Carolina, University of, Library; Division of Health Affairs Library, 289; documents collection, 290; Latin American collection, 291; Hanes Collection, 292; Woman's College Library, 294; Friends of the Library, 295; Southern Historical Collection, 296; Cataloging Department, 414; library instruction in, 431
North Carolina, University of, Library School, 432
Norwalk Public Library, Ohio, 173
Notre Dame, College of, Library, Md., 273
Notre Dame University Library, 462

Oberlin College Library, 310
Ohio Agricultural Experiment Station Library, 357
Ohio State University Library, 308
Ohio Wesleyan University Library, 303
Old Librarians Almanac, 475
Olivia Raney Library, Raleigh, N.C., 126
Oregon, early libraries in, 4, 8
Oregon State Library, 8
Osterhout Free Library, Wilkes-Barre, Pa., 190
Otterbein College Library, 311
Owen, Thomas McAdory, 474

Peabody Institute Library, Baltimore, 365
Peabody Library, Georgetown, D.C., 74
Pearson, Edmund Lester, 475
Penitentiary Libraries, 340; in Ohio, 341
Pennsylvania, early social libraries, 31
Pennsylvania, University of, Library, 313; Fine Arts Library, 317
Pennsylvania Genealogical Society Library, 351
Philadelphia, Free Library of, 188, 191; predecessors of, 129
Philadelphia, Library Company of, 23, 463
Philadelphia Commercial Museum Library, 345
Philosophy of Librarianship, 493
Phoenix College Library, Ariz., 243
Phonograph records, in public libraries, 55
Poole, William Frederick, 461, 467, 476
Pope Pius XII Library, St. Joseph College, Conn., 246
Portage County Library, Ohio, 148
Power, Effie Louise, 477
Pratt Institute Free Library, Brooklyn, 471
Protestant Episcopal Theological Seminary in Virginia Library, 328
Public Library, causal factors, 33